GarageBand
TIPS AND TRICKS

Keith Gemmell

PC Publishing

PC Publishing
Keeper's House
Merton
Thetford
Norfolk IP25 6QH
UK

Tel +44 1953 889900
Fax +44 1953 889901
email info@pc-publishing.com
web site http://www.pc-publishing.com

First published 2007

© Keith Gemmell

ISBN 13: 978 1 870775 19 9

British Library Cataloguing in Publication Data
A catalogue record for this book is available from the British Library

Printed in Great Britain by The Cromwell Press, Trowbridge, Wilts

Contents

Introduction

If you've purchased an Apple Mac computer in the last few years you're probably already familiar with GarageBand, Apple's incredibly easy-to-use, virtual recording studio. Perhaps you're new to recording and dipping your toe in the water. Maybe you're already using this powerful software to write and record your own songs. If you're running version 3, you may even be producing your own radio and video podcasts, using the new jingle content. Whatever your skill-level, one thing's for sure: you're bound to find this book an invaluable working companion.

Okay, the online help and PDF manuals do a fine job of describing how things work. For example, they tell you how to record a Software Instrument and choose a few sounds. But what they don't tell you is that GarageBand's software instruments are the same powerful synthesisers as those found in Logic Pro, only with simplified controls. Once you discover their true potential, there are some powerful editing features just begging to be used. And of course, there are the GarageBand effects. Their origins, too, can be traced back to Logic. Get the low-down here and become a power user.

Some dismiss GarageBand as a toy. But that's just plain silly. Yes it does lack the high-end features of some of the more expensive recording software programs. But rest assured, there are plenty of useful work-arounds and tips and tricks to be had. For those in the know, GarageBand provides all the power tools needed to produce stunning, CD-quality audio projects. Read this book and all will be revealed.

Studio setup and configuration

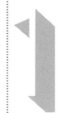

Memory matters

With fast Intel Core Duo processors, all new Macs are inherently capable of running GarageBand with relative ease.

Generally speaking, if you're working with audio you need as much RAM as you can get. 512 MB can now be considered the absolute minimum requirement for running most audio software applications. So if you're buying a new machine, it really is in your best interest to dig a little deeper into your pockets and treat yourself, and your new computer, to extra memory. You won't regret the decision. Of course, if funds are low, you can always install additional memory at a later date.

Speed matters

Apple's notebook computers have slower hard drives (5,400 rpm) than their desktop counterparts (7,200). Although you may get away with recording directly to the internal drives of these machines, you'll get smoother results using an external drive. Choose either a firewire or USB 2 equipped device that functions at a speed of 7,200 rpm.

Driver check

Any third-party audio and MIDI devices that you buy for your Mac will probably come with specially written Core Audio or Core MIDI software drivers. GarageBand looks for these drivers when communicating with the hardware. If they are properly installed, the driver details will appear in the Audio MIDI Setup (AMS), found under Applications > Audio MIDI Setup.

Figure 1.1
Audio setup.

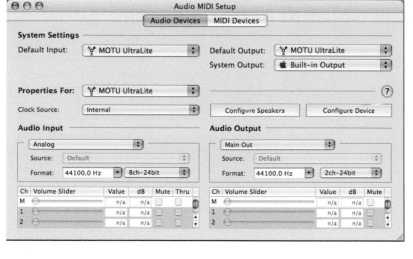

Figure 1.2
MIDI setup.

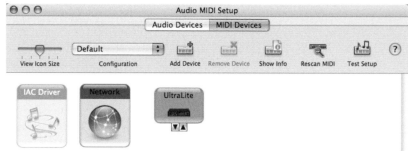

Connection check
In the Audio MIDI Setup utility, ensure that your audio devices are connected and switched on otherwise they won't show up. However, unconnected MIDI devices will appear; they'll just be greyed out.

MIDI scan
When you connect a new MIDI device use the Rescan button in the Audio MIDI Setup to locate it quickly. You can also add the device manually using the Add Device button. Click on a device to rename it. Drag the virtual cables around to connect devices together.

Stop the bleeps
You might like the sounds of croaking frogs and submarines interrupting your music. If you don't, set the System Output to Built-in Output in the Audio MIDI Setup. This will prevent Mac system warnings being played through your audio interface.

A coming together
You can daisy chain audio and MIDI interfaces together in OS X version 10.4 or later. GarageBand will see them as a single device.

Open the Audio/MIDI setup and in the Audio Devices section choose Audio > Open Aggregate Device Editor. Create an aggregate device and rename it. From the list of connected devices, select those you want to use and click 'Done'.

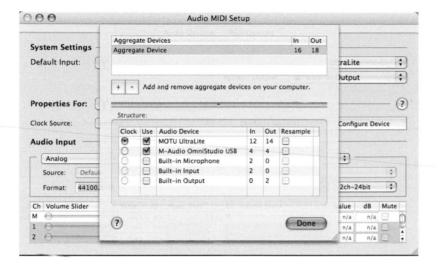

Figure 1.3
Aggregate device.

Buffer sizes - large v small

In more complicated audio software such as Logic Pro and Digital Performer you can set buffer sizes anywhere between 64 and 4096. In GarageBand you only have two choices: large or small. At least it's simple! Choose a small buffer size if you intend playing GarageBand's software instruments with a MIDI keyboard. This will help reduce latency. However, a small buffer size may result in a poor audio performance, particularly if you are recording to several tracks at once. If that's the case, switch to a large buffer size. To set the buffer size, go to GarageBand > Preferences... and choose the Audio/MIDI page.

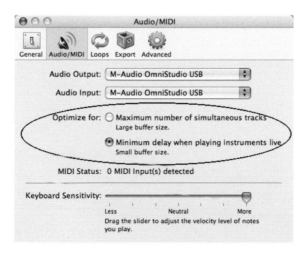

Figure 1.4
Setting buffer size.

Update regularly

If you use third party audio or MIDI hardware, check the manufacturer's website on a regular basis and download the latest drivers. Also, use your Mac's Software Update utility, found in the System Preferences, to keep an eye open for GarageBand updates and bug fixes. You can also check for updates under GarageBand > Check for Updates...

Figure 1.5
Software update is found in the System Preferences.

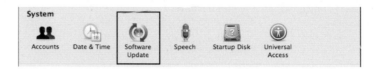

OS updates - think before you act

When a new eye-catching version of Apple's operating system appears on the market it's very tempting to update straightaway. However, before you do, check all relevant third-party manufacturer's websites for driver compatibility. Although most companies are on the case straight away it can sometimes take a few weeks or months for new drivers to appear. Rushing an update may render your audio hardware inoperable for a while. Waiting a bit will most likely save you much wailing and gnashing of teeth.

More speed

GarageBand is a processor hungry program, notorious for forcing even the most powerful computers to their knees. To help prevent this happening to your machine turn off Airport, Bluetooth and all unnecessary programs including Dashboard widgets and anti-virus software.

Preventive maintenance

Occasionally, the OS X user permissions become damaged, which can prevent files and applications from opening. To avoid any possible communication problems between GarageBand and your hard disk it's a good idea to perform this simple maintenance task on a regular basis:

Go to Applications > Utilities and open the Disk Utility program. Select a disk and click Repair Disk. Sit back and wait for the repairs to finish or go make some coffee.

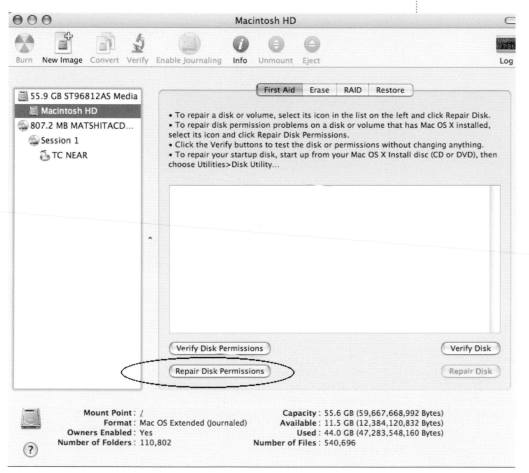

Figure 1.6
Repair the disk regularly to avoid trouble.

Working methods

Any answers?

GarageBand ships with clear easy to understand online help. And further help and support is available at

http://www.apple.com/support/garageband

However, although you can send comments and feedback to Apple at

http://www.apple.com/feedback/garageband.html

you'll not receive any feedback from them. In other words, you can't ask them any questions. So whom can you turn to for help when problems arise?

Fortunately there are many experienced GarageBand users who will happily answer your questions at the Apple Discussions forum. Go to:

http://discussions.apple.com/category.jspa?categoryID=127.

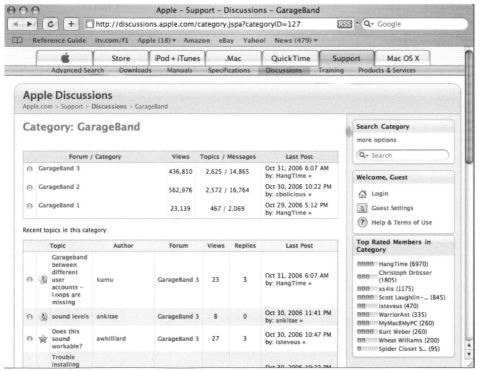

Figure 2.1
AppleDiscussions

7

Any preferences?

Everybody has different ways of working. Unfortunately GarageBand's preferences menu is rather limited. For example, you can't specify pretty colours for your audio tracks like you can in the upmarket sequencers. But you can, among other things, specify default information for exporting your songs, podcasts and movies as well as alter audio buffer sizes, alter your MIDI keyboards sensitivity and specify default audio ins and outs. Go to GarageBand > Preferences and tailor the program to suit you.

Figure 2.2
GarageBand preferences.

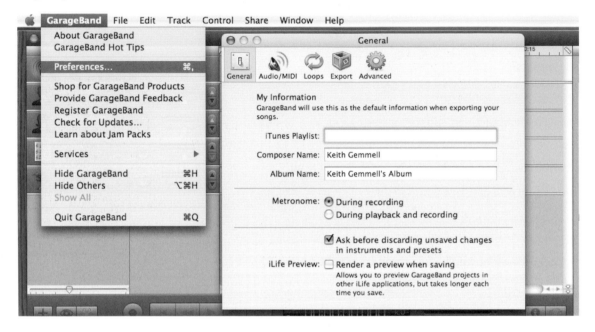

Regular savings

You know it, I know it; all computers, even Macs, crash when you least expect it. Get into the habit of pressing Command-S; you know it makes sense. Yes, I know you've heard this millions of times before but it's worth ramming the message home.

Quite naturally, most musicians become so absorbed in their music making that they completely forget the routine background tasks associated with computers, like saving and making back-ups. So, whenever you record or edit something and you're happy with the result, save it.

Info

GarageBand lets you undo or redo as many actions as you like, since the last time you saved. You can save new versions of your projects at any time by choosing File > Save As.

Backing up

Every so often press Shift-Command-S and save a new, renamed version of your project as a backup. That way, if you reach a point in your work where you don't like what you hear, it's a simple matter of returning to one of the backup files and starting again.

Archive backup

There may be times when you'd like to share your work with others. That's easy enough, isn't it? You just save the project in the normal way and burn it to a CD, right? Not always. Saving your project in the usual way is fine if your project contains just audio files (Real Instrument track recordings that you've recorded yourself). However, if your project contains Apple loops or movie files, doing it this way, they won't be saved.

To ensure that the recipient of your project receives all the media needed to play back your music in full, choose Save As… and then tick the Save as Archive option in the resulting dialogue box.

Figure 2.3
Saving an archive.

Info

GarageBand always references any relevant Apple loops wherever you normally keep them on your computer's hard disk or external drive. If you've recently bought a new Mac, and you haven't moved them, the Apple loops are located at: HD > Library > Audio > Apple Loops > Apple > Apple Loops for GarageBand.

Compact project

If you're working with other GarageBand users across the Internet and you just want to demonstrate a work in progress; why not compact your project when you save it? The audio quality will be reduced but that may not matter if it's just a demo anyway. Use Save As… and tick the Compact Project box. You can choose a degree of compression to suit.

Figure 2.4
Compact Project.

Unpacking project files

Unlike most normal files you save on your Mac, GarageBand project files are not really single files at all; they're packages that actually contain several folders. To get at the contents select a file and control click and hold. Choose Show Package Contents from the resulting menu.

iLife previews

In GarageBand 3 you can save projects as iLife previews. These projects always contain an output folder containing a mixed down stereo audio file. You can then open them in other iLife applications such as iMovie; great if you are into creating multimedia presentations and suchlike. But the real beauty of this feature is that you can also import them back into GarageBand, within an existing GarageBand project. You do this using the new media browser. But of course, the imported project is always a stereo mix-down. You won't get the individual tracks back.

Nevertheless, this is a very useful feature, particularly for creating group mixes. For example, you could use it to create a backing vocal sub-mix, save it (as an iLife preview) and import it into another version of the same song. You will then have your backing vocals on their own pre-mixed stereo track, making the final mix-down much easier to handle.

To save a project as an iLife preview just tick the relevant box in the GarageBand preferences menu. Make sure you save it to Home > Music > GarageBand, otherwise it will not show up in the media browser.

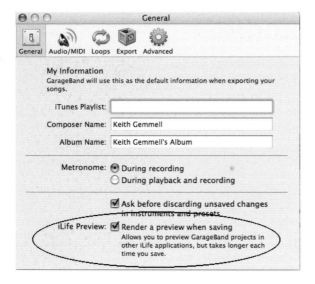

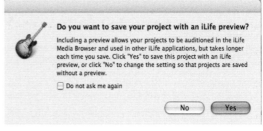

Figure 2.5
Saving with an iLife preview.

To open the file within another GarageBand project, open the Media Browser and select the Audio tab. You will find it in the GarageBand folder.

Figure 2.6
Preview import

Check your output

There is another way to save a mix-down of your project. If you save your songs with the Mastertrack displayed (Command-B) a stereo mix-down is created with the project file. It's saved in an Output folder. You can get at it by showing the package contents (see Unpacking, above). If you leave the Mastertrack hidden, the output file is not created.

Working templates

As a template, the default new music project, complete with a grand piano track and a virtual keyboard, is not very inspiring. Neither is it particularly useful. What's needed is a more personal template, geared to the way you work.

A jazz musician, for example, might like a template that consists of piano, bass and drum software instrument tracks. But a rock musician would probably require a mixture of empty audio tracks (Real Instrument tracks) for guitar, bass and vocals plus a software track for drums. Unfortunately GarageBand doesn't do templates, unless you're into podcasting. So it's a matter of making your own. Here's how it's done.

QuickTip

Because iLife previews contain a complete mix-down of all your audio and software instrument tracks, it takes longer to save them than ordinary project files. For general use, leave the option unchecked in the preferences menu.

QuickTip

When opening projects, using File > Open Recent is often much quicker than trawling through layers of folders to find a project.

1   Open up a blank new music project in GarageBand.

Figure 2.7
Open up a new music project.

2   Delete the piano track (unless you need it, of course) and set up your own personal template.

Figure 2.8
Set up your own template.

3   Save the project.
4   Locate the project file in the Finder.
5   Select the file and choose File > Get Info (Command-I).
6   You'll see two boxes; one marked Stationery Pad the other marked Locked. Tick the Locked box (a padlock appears on the file icon).
7   Double-click the file icon and GarageBand will open your template.

Figure 2.9
Tick the Locked box.

That's it; you now have your own template. Keep it on your desktop and use it to open GarageBand whenever you start a new song.

Because you locked the file, you cannot save the project the first time that you use it (try it and you'll get an error message). Instead, choose File > Save As... and rename the project.

QuickTip

For a smooth workflow, configure items in the Control menu like Metronome and Count In and save them to your template.

Remote control

If you don't enjoy using a mouse to operate transport controls, mixer sliders and knobs you can purchase a remote control device manufactured by M-Audio (www.maudio.co.uk) specifically for GarageBand. Called iControl, you can use it to control all of GarageBand's functions and parameters including EQ and effects parameters. You can also assign its rotary knobs to other Audio Unit plug-ins.

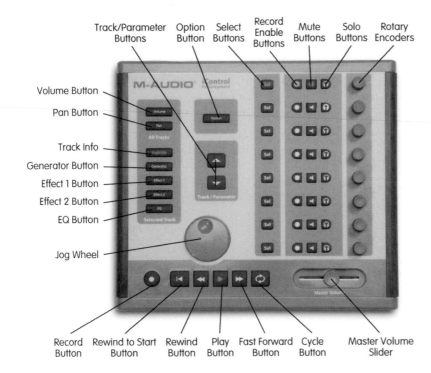

Figure 2.10
iControl remote controller.

Avoid RSI

Constantly using your mouse can lead to RSI (repetitive strain injury). To avoid the problem you might like to investigate alternative solutions. I use a Wacom graphics tablet and pen instead of a mouse (www.wacom.com). For me, holding a pen is much more natural than moving and clicking with a mouse.

Figure 2.11
Use a graphics tablet to reduce the risk of RSI.

Info

If you suffer from repetitive strain when using your mouse do an Internet search. Type 'alternative mouse' or 'ergonomic mouse' into a search engine and you'll find there are plenty of alternatives. Be prepared for a few whacky ones though.

Keyboard shortcuts

There are keyboard shortcuts for most menus and quite a few more for various functions. But remembering them all is quite a formidable task. Here are a few of the most important key commands that you'll need (a more comprehensive list can be found on page 109).

- Play or Stop – Space bar
- Fast forward – Hold down the right arrow (press and release for one bar increments)
- Rewind – Hold down the left arrow (press and release for one bar increments)
- Record – R
- Cycle on/off – C
- Return to zero – Z or Return (same as Enter)
- Metronome on/off – Command-U
- Count in on/off – Command-Shift-U

More screen space

With everything happening in a single window, GarageBand tends to hog screen space. This is especially true of version 3, which can only be resized by a small amount. To avoid clicking on icons in the dock, and accidentally opening other programs, hide the dock. In the Finder, choose Dock > Turn Hiding On. Alternatively turn it on and off using the keyboard shortcut Alt-Command-D.

You can also hide and show the dock automatically by opening the Dock Preferences and ticking the relevant box.

Figure 2.12
Dock Preferences.

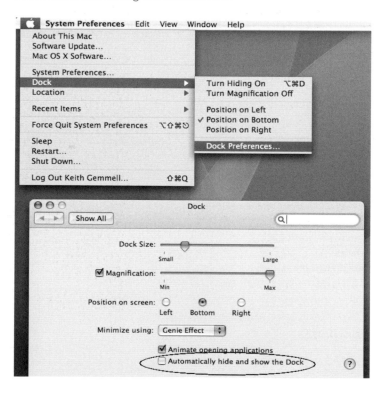

Big Ed

In its default size, the editor window is a bit on the tiny side. To make it larger, grab the dividing line and move it upwards. That's so much better, especially for MIDI note editing, either as bars or notes.

Figure 2.13
Move the dividing line on the editor window up to give yourself more space for editing bars or notes.

Marking time

The posher audio sequencers out there contain useful marker tracks, for marking out verses, choruses and other meaningful points in a musical composition. Unfortunately GarageBand versions one and two don't contain marker tracks. But there is a way round this and you can create your own. Here's how to mark up a song's intro, verse and chorus.

1 Create a software instrument track or use the default grand piano track that appears when you open a new music project.
2 Command-Click in the track, to create a new empty region.
3 Select the empty region, open the editor and rename it as Intro.
4 Resize the region to fit the length of your intro, fours bars maybe.

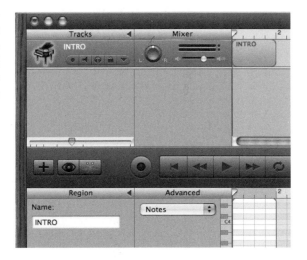

Figure 2.14
Renaming a region.

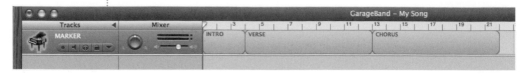

Figure 2.15
Create more regions and rename them.

5 Use copy and paste to create two more identical regions, starting at bar 5.
6 Resize the new regions, to suit, and rename them as Verse and Chorus.

In version 3, making a marker track is even easier. Here's how to mark up a song's intro, verse and chorus.

1 Create a podcast track. It appears, conveniently, as the first track. In fact it can't be moved anyway.

Figure 2.16
Create a podcast track.

2 Place the playhead at the start of bar 1.
3 Select the podcast track and open the editor.
4 Click on the Add Marker button. A blue line containing marker information appears.
5 Alter the words Chapter Title to read Intro.

Figure 2.17
Alter the words
Chapter Title to
read Intro .

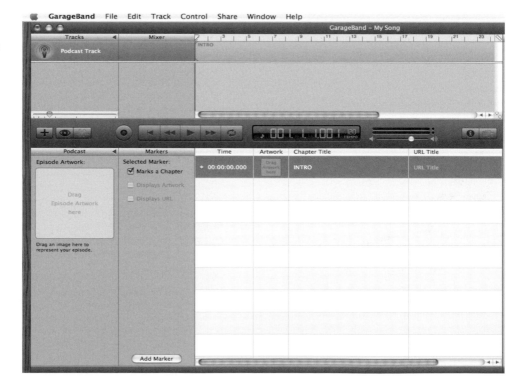

6 Move the playhead to another position in the timeline, four bars on perhaps, and add another marker. Rename it Verse.

7 Continue to add markers for choruses, verses and bridges as and where you need them.

Figure 2.18
Add markers for choruses, verses and bridges as and where you need them.

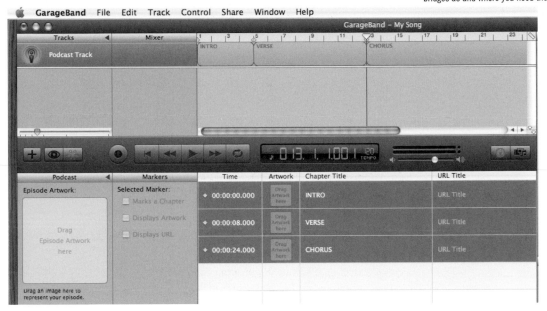

CPU watch

Another feature that the up-market sequencers have is a system performance meter for measuring how much of your computer's processing power is being used to play a project. GarageBand doesn't have a dedicated meter for this. However, you can get a fair idea of how your computer is coping by keeping an eye on the playhead. It changes colour from yellow through orange to red. Yellow indicates moderate processor use and orange indicates high processor use. If it glows red your project is close to overloading the processor.

Apple loops

Bigger browser

When you open the loop browser, by default, 30 buttons appear (a row of six horizontal ones and a vertical column of five). To widen your options, linger with your mouse just to left of the record button or to the right of the master volume slider. The mouse pointer changes to a hand, which you can use to drag the dark grey dividing bar upwards, complete with transport controls. This will expose a further six vertical columns giving you a total of 11. That gives you a grand total of 66 available buttons to work with.

Figure 3.1
See more loop buttons.

Loops for pitch shifters

If you're into outrageous pitch shifting go to the Loops section of the GarageBand preferences and uncheck the Keyword Browsing box. By default, GarageBand limits your search to loops that are within two semitones of your song's key. And there's a good reason for that, of course. By and large, conventional instrument loops will sound strange if they are pitch shifted much beyond a few semitones. Most of the Apple loops supplied with GarageBand fall into the conventional cat-

Figure 3.2
Un-check the Keyword box to widen your options when searching for loops to pitch shift.

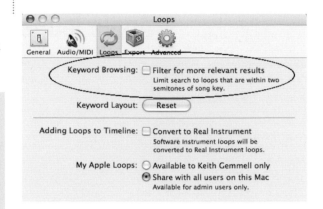

QuickTip

You can find loops quickly using the loop browser search facility. For example, to instantly locate a selection of Fusion Electric Piano loops, type the words 'fusion electric piano' and press 'enter'.

QuickTip

Don't forget the small arrows at the top of the loop browser; they're easily overlooked. You can use these arrows to manage which loop folders you want displayed.

egory. However, for dance and electronic tracks extreme pitch shifting is very common. Un-checking the Keyword box is going to widen your options considerably when searching for loops to pitch shift.

When you're searching the loop browser and you come across a loop that you really like, add it to your favourites list (tick the Fav box, in the results list. To view all your favourites in the results list, click the Favorites keyword button, in button view. Alternatively, select the Favorites keyword type in column view.

Figure 3.3
Select your favourite loops.

Figure 3.4
Favourites in column view.

Time signature warning!

If you choose a time signature other than 4/4, 3/4 or 6/8 when you create a new song, be aware that you won't be able to include Apple loops in your song. Choose 2/4, for example (a common enough time signature), and all the buttons in the loop browser will be greyed out. Fortunately most popular music is in 4/4-time so it's not a major problem.

Search by scale type

We've already discussed searching for loops with or without pitch shifting options (see Loops for pitch shifters, page 19). But selecting loops that fit the scale type of your songs – major or minor – is also important. Some major scale loops will not fit with other minor scale loops and vice versa, for obvious musical reasons. Some, however, will fit both. Use the pop-up Scale menu in the loop browser to choose your search options.

Figure 3.5
Searching for scale types.

Turn green loops into blue loops

Just to clear up any confusion about the difference between blue and green Apple loops:

Real instrument loops (audio loops) are coloured blue. They are recordings of a real instrumentalist or vocalist playing a real instrument (the human voice is an instrument, is it not?). You can edit these loops to a limited extent but you can't change the individual notes that were played without using a pretty fancy external audio editor.

Figure 3.6
Editing audio loops.

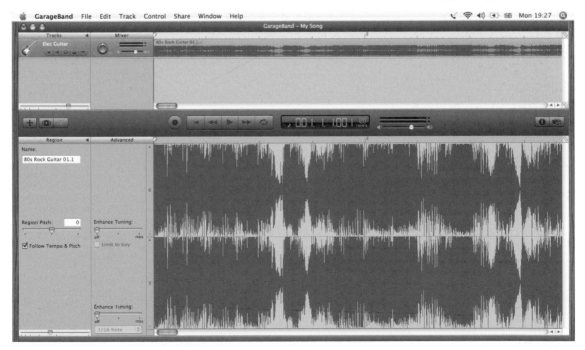

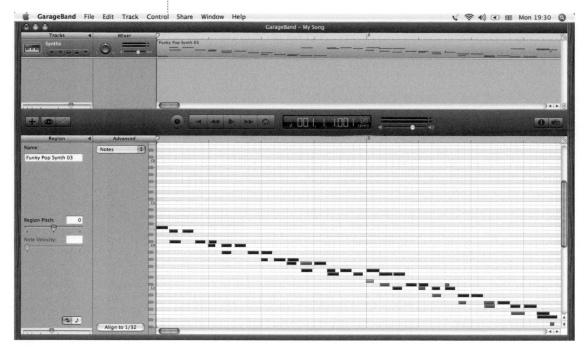

Figure 3.7
MIDI loops can be edited easily.

Software instrument loops (MIDI loops) are coloured green. As you've probably discovered, MIDI loops contain note and controller data that can be easily manipulated and edited. They can also be assigned to different software instruments.

But did you know that MIDI loops could also be rendered as audio loops? In other words, turned from green to blue.

To turn a green loop into a blue loop just option-drag it onto the timeline, in an empty space. An audio track will be created and the MIDI loop becomes an audio loop.

Also worth knowing, if you just drag (not option-drag) a MIDI loop onto to an audio track it will be converted to an audio loop (again, green to blue).

But why bother changing the format anyway, if both loop types sound the same? Well, audio loops use less of your computer's processing power than do software instruments. Also, you might want to edit the loop in ways not available in MIDI loop format.

Info

If you want to convert software instrument loops (green) into real instrument loops (blue) whenever you load them, go to Preferences > Loops and tick the appropriate box.

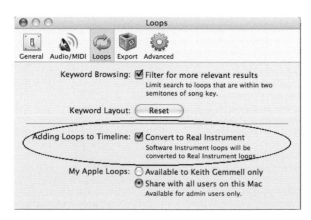

Figure 3.8
Converting a MIDI loop to an audio loop.

Identical loops sound different

If you've converted a green MIDI loop to a blue audio loop it may sound slightly different. This is down to time stretching. In most cases the difference is barely noticeable but it's worth knowing about. Load the loop in both MIDI and audio formats and check them side-by-side if the audio version sounds strange.

Sharing tracks

As mentioned above, you can drag MIDI loops to audio tracks and they will be converted to audio loops. This means that you can juxtapose a whole load of different instrument loops on a single track, to conserve CPU usage. For example, you could have an electric piano loop followed by a horn section loop followed by a string loop.

It's a great work-around if your computer is under strain, but this method of working does have its drawbacks. For a start, each loop will probably require some volume and pan adjustment when it comes to mix-down. But that can be fixed by using the track automation features.

Of more concern are the effects that you may have assigned to the track. You can't alter these mid-track, which means all the loops will be treated with the same effects; in all likelihood, not what you want.

Consider the example above, electric piano followed by horns and strings on the same audio track. It's likely that the electric piano will employ an effect of some kind – phasing perhaps. This will sound inappropriate on the horns and strings. So the trick is to use shared tracks only for loops that don't need effects at all or for those that will benefit from the same effect.

Sharing tracks is very useful when you need to conserve your computer's resources, although the freeze tracks function in GarageBand 2 and 3 is probably a better way to save on CPU usage. Having said that; if effects are not a consideration it's a neat and easy way to manage a series of loops without using up too much screen space.

Home-grown loops

If you've read the GarageBand online help you probably already know that you can save your own recorded audio and MIDI performances as Apple loops. It's done by selecting a region and choosing Edit > Add To Loop Library. You're then presented with the Add Loop dialogue, which gives you a variety of options for tagging the new loop. You can choose the scale and genre, instrument category, instrument range and mood description. The loop turns blue, to indicate that it's an Apple Loop, and is added to the loop browser.

This is a great feature and it works very well. However, the Add Loop facility is really just a cut down version of the Apple Loops Utility. A free application for professional Apple Loop developers, the Apple Loops Utility provides more advanced features.

As well as being able to create the tags mentioned above, with the Add Loops feature, the Apple Loops Utility allows you to create time signatures. The main reason for using it, though, is that it allows you to create transient markers. These are created automatically when you create Apple Loops with-

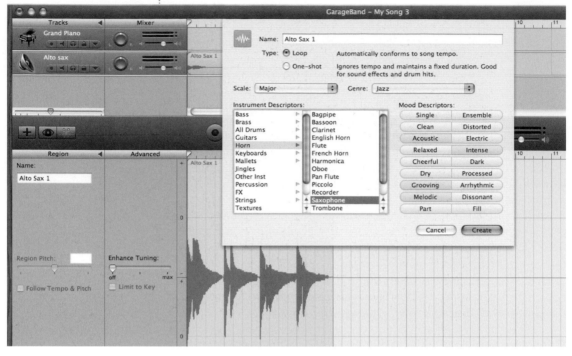

Figure 3.9
The Add Loop dialogue.

in GarageBand. But the Apple Loops Utility gives you much more control over the process. In many cases, loops that are properly created with the Apple Loops Utility will perform much better when subjected to tempo and pitch shifting adjustments.

Info

The Apple Loops Utility will import WAV as well as AIFF files.

Info

Apple discourages people like me from disclosing the download URL for the Apple Loops Utility. However, if you want to supercharge your homegrown loop making just type the words Apple Loops Utility into Google and you'll find it soon enough. An 18-page user manual is included in the download.

Setting transient markers in the Apple Loops Utility

If you're working with rhythmic material listen carefully to the beats and choose your transient setting accordingly; transient settings of 1/8-notes and 1/16- notes generally work best. Slide the sensitivity slider to the right to detect more transients.

Larger transient settings usually work best with melodic material. If the audio contains a fluid passage then settings of 1/8-notes or 1/4-notes are likely to be the most suitable. Melodic material with small transient settings of 1/16-note and above will sound jittery when they are slowed down.

If you've added too many transients with the sensitivity slider you can delete some of them by selecting and hitting the backspace key. Alternatively, drag a triangle off the interface.

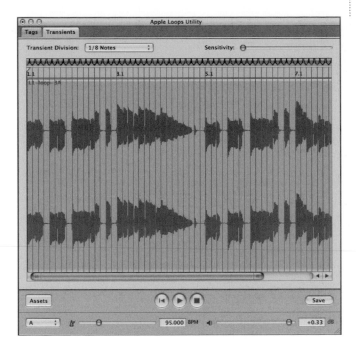

Figure 3.10
Transient settings.

The trick to getting things right is to test each file at various tempos, using the tempo slider. Most will sound strange if you reduce the tempo by about half. However, doing so and tweaking the transients at a slow tempo will yield the best results when less drastic tempo changes are made later in GarageBand.

Audio recording

Preferences check

Before you embark on recording audio tracks it's a good idea to check GarageBand's audio inputs and outputs. Open the preferences and click the Audio/MIDI tab. If you have an audio interface connected to your computer it appears here, in the pop-up menu, alongside the built-in audio options.

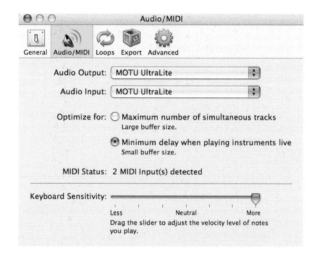

Figure 4.1
Audio and MIDI Preferences.

Built-in microphone

Most modern Apple Mac computers feature a built-in microphone. While you'll not get top-quality audio, with care, acceptable results are possible. In fact, for songwriters, it makes an ideal tool for capturing ideas quickly, just about anywhere, if you have a Macbook or Macbook Pro.

Place yourself at a reasonably close distance to your computer screen and speak or sing into the microphone. As you do so, check the signal level in the track mixer. If the signal is too high (hitting red) or too low, use the volume slider in the track info window, not the slider in the track mixer, to adjust the volume.

Figure 4.2
Adjust the mic volume in the track info window...

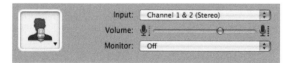

Figure 4.3
... or use the internal microphone volume sliders.

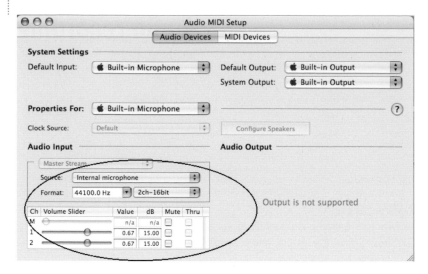

You can also use the internal microphone volume sliders (one for each input) in the OS X Audio/MIDI setup.

Reducing background noise

When using your computers built-in microphone for speech or singing, use the ambient noise reduction feature found in the System Sound Preferences window. This will help to eliminate any background noise in the room. It won't exactly mask the sound of the men drilling the road outside your studio window but it will prevent the sound of your squeaky chair leaking onto your recordings.

Figure 4.4
Reduce ambient noise in the System Sound Preferences window.

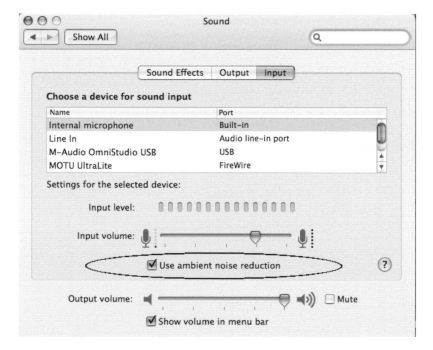

Silent mic

If you're trying to record with your Mac's built-in microphone and you're not getting a signal, open the preferences, click the Audio/MIDI tab and select Built-in Microphone as the audio input.

Also, open the Sound preferences window (found under System preferences) and check the inputs and outputs found there – see the previous screenshot. While you're there, if necessary, adjust the microphone input level using the slider provided. A mid-way setting is usually okay but will vary, naturally, with the loudness of your voice.

Stereo to mono

If you're starting from scratch with a new music project, you'll need to create a blank audio track to record onto. In GarageBand new audio tracks are, rather confusingly, called Real Instrument tracks. And what's more, they are set to record in stereo by default, which is not what we usually need.

Figure 4.5
Mono or stereo?

Of course, if you were planning to record an instrument in stereo, a synthesizer perhaps, you would simply leave the track info window settings as they appear by default; the input channels would display 1/2.

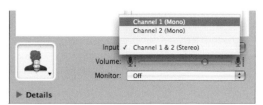

But vocals and most acoustic instruments are commonly recorded onto mono tracks. So before you rush into recording your voice or guitar, check the track info window and alter the settings accordingly.

If your intention is to record in mono and you do forget to change the track to stereo, you'll see two identical waveforms, one above the other, appearing in the region as you record. This is effectively doubling the size of your audio file and wasting disk space. Switch the track to mono and rerecord the audio and you'll see just a single waveform forming in the region.

Figure 4.6
This track contains a stereo region.

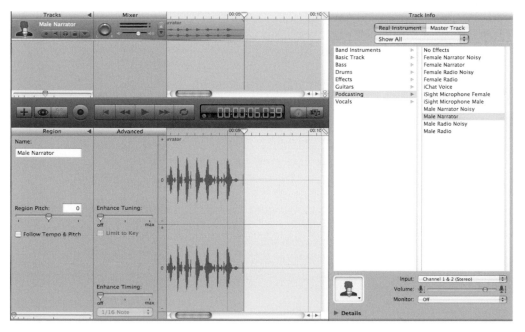

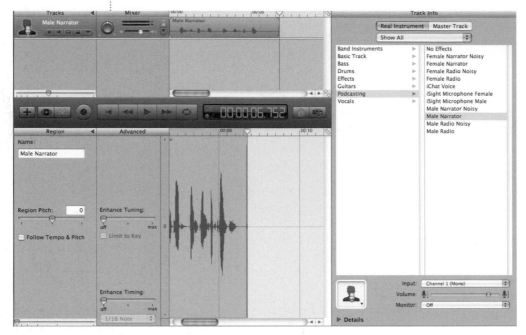

Figure 4.7
This track contains a mono region.

Avoid the red light area

If you've ever used an analogue tape recorder you'll know that it's possible to occasionally drive the record levels into the red without fear of distortion. On analogue tape this amounts to a form of compression and can provide a bigger, 'warmer' sound. However, try it on a digital recorder and you'll end up with nothing of the sort – just distortion. By all means keep as close to the red area as possible but be careful never to exceed it.

Your own input

Newcomers to GarageBand often, mistakenly, assume that when recording, you set the input signal levels using the track mixer volume slider. Of course, if you think about it, this can't be so. The volume slider only affects the play-back of the audio once it's recorded. So when recording, remember, the level meters show the signal level at the 'input' selected for the audio channel. You can adjust this level in one of the following ways:

- By adjusting the output level of the sound source (guitar, vocal or whatever) or your external mixer.
- If you're using the computers built-in audio inputs, by adjusting the volume slider in the track info window.
- By using your audio hardware's own software mixer to set the input levels, if this is provided. The MOTU Ultralite audio interface, for example, has its own software called a CueMix Console.

Multitrack confusion

A frequently asked question – I thought that GarageBand recorded several tracks at a time, like a conventional stand-alone hardware recorder. I can't get this to work. How is it done?

You can record up to eight audio tracks (Real Instrument tracks) and a single MIDI track (Software Instrument track) simultaneously. In theory, then, you could record a vocalist and backing band at once; or for that matter, any other kind of instrumental or vocal ensemble. However, the main limitation to doing so is your audio hardware.

If you have a stereo sound card or audio interface, then only two inputs will show up in the Audio/MIDI preferences window. In this case you can only record two sound sources at once (although a single source may contain a mix of different instruments or voices) and further overdubbing will probably be required.

If you have a multi-input card or interface, any amount of inputs (depending on the hardware) will show up in the Audio/MIDI window.

When GarageBand first appeared, recording was limited to just two tracks. For that reason buying a multi-input audio interface was considered overkill. In fact, GarageBand was, at that time, pretty much considered a toy. But now

Figure 4.8
Use your own software mixer to adjust input levels. This is the MOTU Ultralite Mixer.

Figure 4.9
The M-Audio FastTrack USB is an ideal interface for singer/songwriters working with GarageBand. It features an input for instruments like guitar, bass and keyboards, plus a microphone input for recording vocals or other acoustic sounds.

Figure 4.10
The Samson C01U is one of many good quality Chinese microphones now available at very reasonable prices. No audio interface is required with the C01U; just plug it into one of your computer's USB ports.

Figure 4.11
Use a pop shield. It also keeps vocalists from getting too close to the mic. This is the Samson PS-01.

with nine simultaneous track recording available it's worth splashing out on a good quality interface, particularly if you want to record a complete band.

Recording vocals

To record vocals properly you'll need a directional microphone. A condenser type is best. Companies like AKG produce a range to suit most pockets but there are also quite a few cheap, but decent, Chinese condenser models around these days. By and large, they've replaced the trusty Shure SM58 as the budget microphone of choice in the project studio.

Although some microphones have built-in windshields, it's always a good idea to use a pop shield. Apart from minimising the effects of sudden, explosive blasts of air, it will also keep vocalists from singing too close to the microphone.

A distance of around 60 cm between the mouth and the microphone is usual with the microphone tilted slightly, either up or down, away from a direct line with the mouth. A greater distance is fine but bear in mind the fact that more gain may be needed if the vocalist has a quiet voice. Problems with background noise could also arise. Keep the microphone away from reflective surfaces, walls being an obvious example.

Recording electric guitars

Small practice amplifiers are ideal for recording guitars but the sound is reflected off the floor and colours the tone. The answer – place the amplifier on a chair, half a metre or so above the ground.

A dynamic microphone such as the Shure SM57 or SM58 is an ideal choice for the job. To begin with, place it between 15 and 30 cm from the centre of one of the speakers in the amplifier cabinet. Experiment by moving it off centre from there, to achieve a desirable tone. Try using two microphones, one further away or at the side, or even behind the speaker cabinet. Use a similar method for bass guitar but place it further away, to avoid a boxy sound. Alternatively, record the bass direct.

Amp simulation

If you're not happy mic'ing up your guitar amplifier (or perhaps you don't have one) you can always take advantage of the various amplifier types generated by GarageBand's Amp Simulation. It's certainly a whole lot simpler and you can edit the settings afterwards. The guitar is actually recorded 'dry' without the effect.

The easiest way to get started is use one of the presets found in the track info window and to edit them to suit your own style. There are plenty to choose from and the chances are that you'll soon find something that suits.

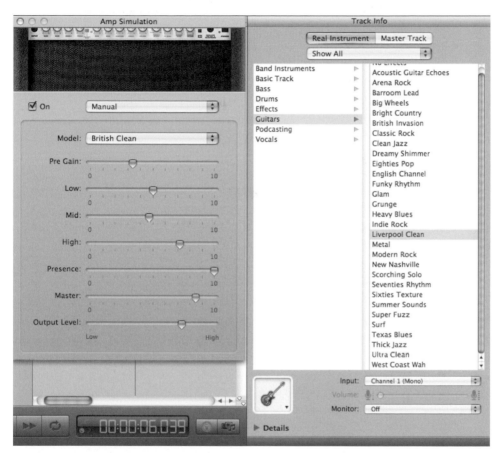

Figure 4.12
Pick your own guitar preset.

Working with the presets is fine but you will probably find it more musically satisfying to devise your own guitar set-up based on one of GarageBand's virtual amplifiers. There are four basic types:

- American Gain – modelled on the Mesa amps, which feature separate preamp and power amp controls. Good for modern rock and grunge sounds.
- American Clean – modelled on the great Fender amps of yesteryear, notable for their rich detailed sound. Good for authentic rock 'n' roll, country and blues.

- British Gain – modelled on the ubiquitous Marshall stack made famous by the likes of Jimi Hendrix, Jimmy Page and Ritchie Blackmoore who pioneered the famous overdriven hard rock sound. Good for heavy metal, classic lead guitar solos and indie rock.
- British Clean – modelled on the early Vox amps used by the Beatles and countless other British beat-groups of the nineteen-sixties. Good for rhythm guitar and general pop music styles.

Figure 4.13
Amp simulation.

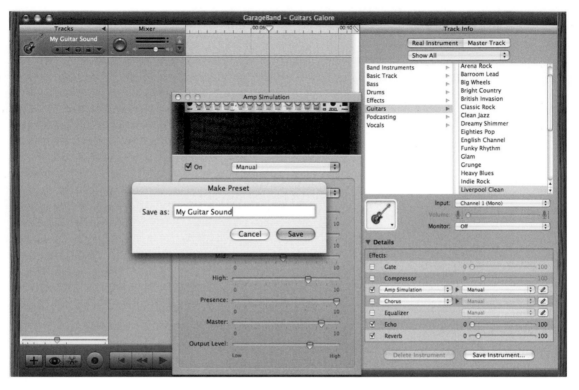

Setting up a rig of your own is easy

Create a basic track without effects. Open the track info window and click the Details triangle. Select Amp Simulation in the first available effects slot. Leaving the preset as Manual, click the pencil icon and off you go.

How you set things up from here depends very much on the style of music you're recording and which type of guitar you play.

Use the pre gain slider to add distortion, just as you might with a real guitar amp. The low, mid and high controls are used for tone shaping.

The presence parameter further emphasises the high end, allowing the processed signal to really cut through a mix.

Recording acoustic guitars

Nylon string guitars are not loud instruments. For best results you'll need a sensitive microphone to record them properly, preferably a condenser with a flat frequency response.

Aim the microphone somewhere between the sound hole and the end of the neck, but keep your distance, maybe as far as 45 cm.

QuickTip

The amp simulation feature works just as well on bass as it does on guitar. Try it with keyboards, too.

If you're a singer-songwriter you will probably prefer to record guitar and vocals together. Tilt the vocal microphone upwards a little and the guitar microphone down, to avoid phase cancelled signals.

To capture the richness of good acoustic guitar, try seating the player in a room with a reflective floor – wood or stone, as opposed to carpet. Alternatively, place a large piece of wood under the chair (assuming the player is sitting down).

Recording brass and saxophones

Brass instruments produce high sound pressure levels (SPL) so choose your microphone carefully. Condensers with a large diaphragm and a flat frequency response are best. If the microphone has an attenuation switch, use it to cope with the inevitable high sound pressure levels.

Good quality dynamic microphones such as the SM 58 and the Sennheiser MD series will also make a good job of recording brass and saxophones without the worry of high SPL.

Place the microphone slightly off axis to the bell when recording trumpets and trombones. That's because although higher frequencies are projected in front of the bell, the lower ones are spread over a wider area.

When recording saxophones place the microphone over and above the tone holes, not directly over the bell. Although some of the sound emanates from the bell a good deal of it also escapes from the tone holes.

Recording woodwind

A large diaphragm condenser is the best microphone choice for recording flutes, clarinets and other wind instruments. Wind instrument design varies considerably and the trick to obtaining a good overall sound is to find out where the main sound source lies. For example, like the saxophone, a clarinet has a bell and a series of tone holes. Actually, most of the sound emanates from the tone holes and the only time all the sound escapes from the bell is when all the holes are closed. So the best microphone position is above the clarinet.

When recording the flute the microphone is usually placed above the instrument, towards the mouthpiece.

If you're not sure where to place the microphone when recording a wind instrument, ask the player. They almost always know the best spot.

Recording strings

Recording a violin can be tricky. For a start, violinists tend to move around a lot. Ask the player to sit down. This also helps reflections from the ceiling. Use a flat response cardoid microphone placed over the bridge. The distance depends on the style of music and the type of sound you want. Basically, the closer you go, the scratchier it gets.

Small string ensembles are easy to record. Use a crossed pair of mics (at right angles to each other) above the players.

Recording grand piano

Most musicians have neither the space nor the money for a grand piano in their home studio. If you're one of the lucky few, place a condenser microphone about 50 cm above the bass strings and another, the same distance above the treble strings.

Recording upright piano

The average musician is more likely to have a beer stained upright in the corner of his studio than a full size grand piano. If that's you, open the lid and place two directional condensers, one at each end, above the treble and bass strings. If that doesn't work, take off the front panel and place the mics in front of the strings.

Monitor your input

When recording into GarageBand you will need to:

* Hear what you are recording
* Hear the existing recorded tracks
* Hear any GarageBand effects on the track you're recording

The process is known as 'monitoring'. Basically, there are two ways to do it:

Monitoring through GarageBand

To hear the input signal along with effects, monitoring via GarageBand is the way to go. Using this method, the input signal is mixed with the audio playback. This is ideal if you like touches of reverb on your voice or you need to hear a certain effect on your guitar while you are recording. All you have to do is turn monitoring on in the track info window.

Figure 4.14
Turn monitoring on in the track info window.

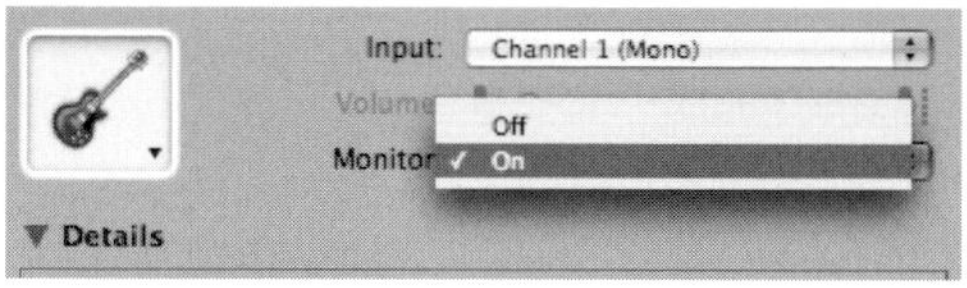

There is a drawback to monitoring through GarageBand – latency. The signal you hear back will be slightly delayed. It might not be much but even a delay of 20 milliseconds or so can be very off-putting to most musicians. The latency value depends on your audio hardware and drivers and it's usually possible to lower them by choosing the small buffer size option in the Audio/MIDI preferences (Preferences > Audio/MIDI).

Having said that; if you own one of the latest Apple Mac computers with fast Intel core-duo processors you will not have much of a latency problem.

Monitoring through your audio hardware

If you are using an audio interface, you may be able to use direct monitoring. The interface handles the monitoring and routes the input signal to GarageBand as well as directly to a headphone output. This method will provide you with zero latency.

The drawback to monitoring this way, however, is that you won't be able to hear any GargeBand effects on the track you're recording; reverb on vocals or amp simulation on guitar, for example. That's because the input signal doesn't actually pass through GarageBand. You will, of course, be able to hear any effects applied to the previously recorded tracks. If you record this way, turn off the monitoring option in GarageBand's track info window.

Another way to monitor your performance is to use a small hardware mixer. This way the input signal can be treated with an effect and sent to your main studio monitor speakers or headphones. An additional feed, without the effect, is then sent from the auxiliary sends on the mixer to your audio interface. If the mixer has direct channel outputs use those instead. If you record this way, again, turn off GarageBand's monitoring in the track info window.

Audio monitoring stops working

Using two audio interfaces, one for input and another for output, is likely to cause problems on versions of GarageBand earlier than 3.0. Clicks and pops are heard and after about 90 seconds, audio monitoring packs up altogether. The most likely scenario is when an external USB or FireWire audio interface is used for input and your computer's built-in audio for output. The solution: use just one interface.

Patching up mistakes – punching in and out

If you've made a mistake in the middle of an otherwise perfect take, don't despair. You don't necessarily have to record it all again. Punch-in and punch-out recording is the answer. You can do this manually but that's not so easy if you're working alone, particularly if you're an instrumentalist. For example, I'm a saxophone player and playing a part and diving across the room to start and stop recording is a hazardous business with a tenor sax slung round your neck, believe me. So I automate the process using cycle record. Here's how it's done.

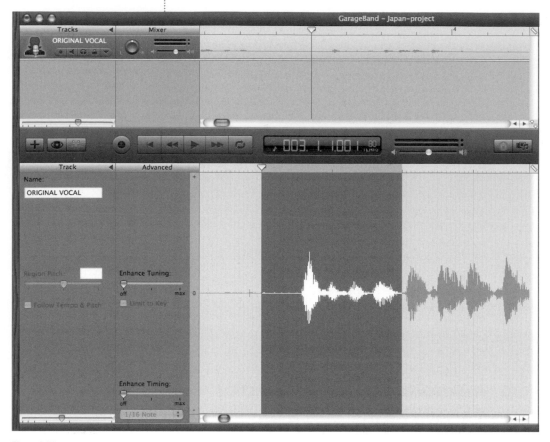

Figure 4.15
A short vocal passage is marked for replacement

1 Ensure that the count-in and metronome are turned on.
2 Set up a cycle that encompasses the audio you want to replace.
   Remember, the grid setting is directly related to the playhead position so
   adjust it accordingly.
3 Start recording and play after the count-in.

GarageBand will start recording at the beginning of the cycle and stop
recording at the end. Your previously recorded audio is erased and replaced
with the newly recorded material. The cycle continues (you'll hear your new
material) until you press stop.

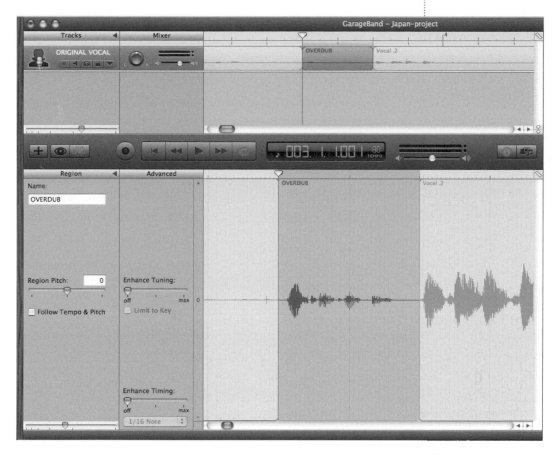

Patching up mistakes – without punching in and out

There's no doubt that as far as digital recording is concerned, punch in and out recording is fast becoming an obsolete method of repairing recorded tracks. Isolating mistakes, muting them and re-recording the material on new tracks make for an easier way to patch up a flawed performance. Here's how it's done:

1   Duplicate a couple of extra tracks (Command-D). Isolate the audio that you want to replace using the split feature (Command-T) to create a new region.

Figure 4.16
A cycle region is set up to encompass the mistakes and the track is repaired using punch in and out recording.

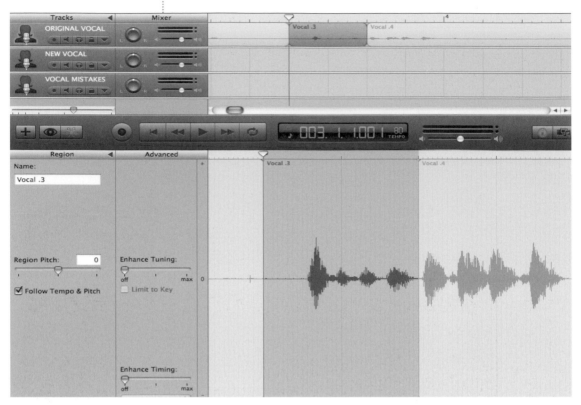

Figure 4.17
Create a new region.

2 Drag the new region to one of the new tracks (be careful not to move it forwards or backwards in time). You can't mute the new region so mute the track.

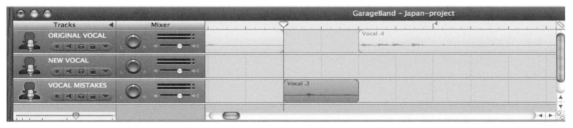

Figure 4.18
Discarded audio.

3 Now record a new take on the remaining empty track.

Figure 4.19
Record a new take.

4 Trim it and slot it into the original track (or simply leave it where it is).

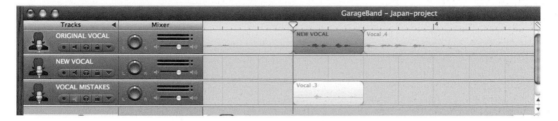

Figure 4.20

Locking tracks

Working with audio puts quite a strain on your computer's resources. One way to free up CPU is to lock your completed audio tracks. It couldn't be simpler but people often forget to do it and struggle on with jerky playback and intermittent stops. Just click the padlock icon in the track pane. An audio file is rendered to your hard drive, which plays back as normal. You can't edit it, though, until you unlock the track by clicking the icon again.

Figure 4.21

QuickTip

Locking a track is neat method of rendering both MIDI software instrument tracks and audio tracks to your hard drive ready for processing in an external audio editor.

Audio editing

Cut and paste

Cutting and pasting sections of audio is a commonly used technique in music production. Now, I'm a great advocate of repetition in music, but normally, only if there is variation of some kind. To record a lead vocal chorus and paste it repeatedly through a song is not usually a good idea. You run the risk of losing your listener's interest.

However, recording, cutting and pasting a backing vocal section is fine because your audience will mostly be listening to the lead vocal. They're unlikely to notice the repetition happening in the background.

In the end, it's down to musical style, taste and common sense. Use it where it's going to save you time.

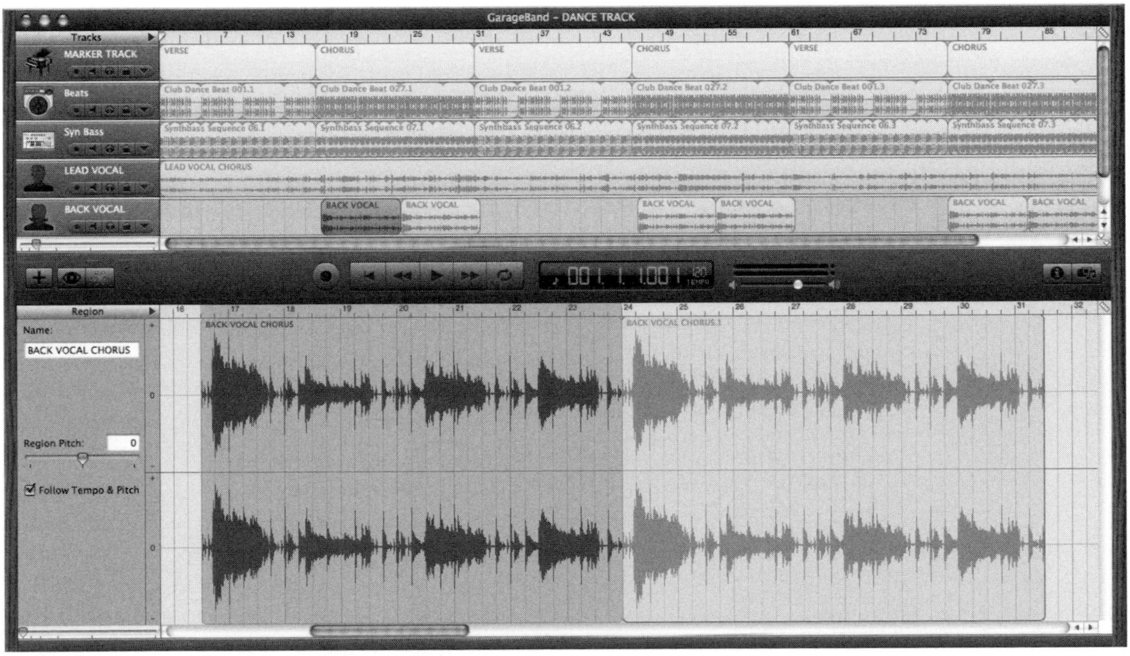

Figure 5.1
A cut and paste vocal.

Comping

This technique has been around since the dawn of multi-track recording. It's mostly used for lead vocals and instrumental solos. In the old days of analogue tape recording the singer would record two or three versions of a song onto different tracks. Afterwards, the producer and vocalist would select the best bits from each. The engineer would then bounce those sections down to a single 'composite' track.

You can do the same thing in GarageBand. Record a few versions of, let's say, a vocal song chorus onto adjacent audio tracks. Audition each track in turn, sort out the best bits and cut and paste them to a new, empty audio track. Be sure to keep them in the same place on the timeline.

Figure 5.2
Comping vocal takes.

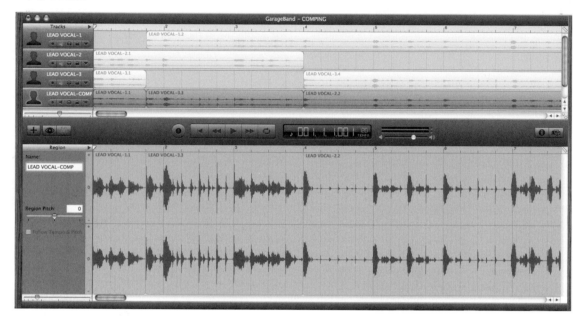

Editing outside of GarageBand

Audio editing is somewhat limited in GarageBand (after all, it is supplied free when you buy a new Apple Mac computer). But that doesn't necessarily mean that you can't perform complex editing procedures using an external editor. But how do you access the audio files you need to edit?

Locate the project file (.band file) that you're working on and control-click it. Choose the Show Package Contents option. Look in the Media fold-

Figure 5.3
Choose the Show Package Contents option.

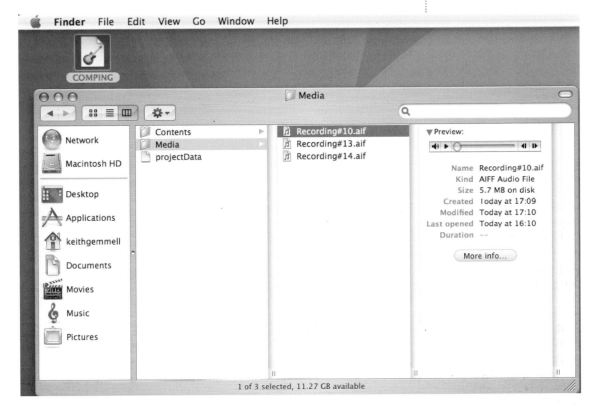

Figure 5.4
Audition the files if necessary.

er and you will find all your audio files. Drag copies of those you need onto the desktop and rename them. Audition them with the OSX preview player if you're not sure which is which.

The audacity of it

The music industry standard for audio editing on the Apple Mac these days is Bias Peak Pro (www.bias-inc.com). The full version will set you back $600 and the light version about $130. Apple's Soundtrack Pro also includes an audio editing suite. But let's face it; if you're a GarageBand user, buying these products is overkill. Your money would be better spent upgrading to another sequencing package such as Logic Express.

So does this mean that GarageBand users can't perform any pro-style audio editing at all? By no means, just go to http://audacity.sourceforge.net and download a free copy of Audacity, an easy-to-use basic audio editor. Once you have imported an audio file into Audacity you can make some radical changes to your files that are impossible in GarageBand.

Here are some of the most useful and commonly used functions of Audacity:

QuickTip

When working on your audio files in an audio editor outside of GarageBand be sure to work on copies and keep the original intact. Otherwise, once you've made changes there is no going back.

- *Using the drawing tool* You've recorded a first-class take in GarageBand but there's a slight click or pop amongst the audio. The noise is smack bang in the middle of a waveform and you can't remove it in GarageBand's audio editor without spoiling the take. Once the file is in Audacity you can zoom in on the waveform and remove it with the drawing tool.

Figure 5.5
Identify the spike...

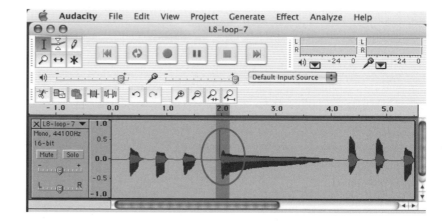

Figure 5.6
Zoom in until you see the individual samples and use the drawing tool to remove the spike (redraw)

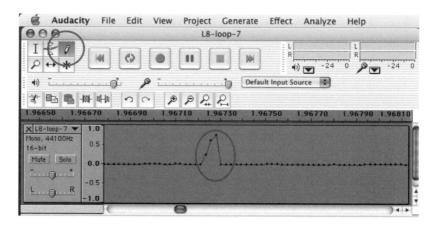

Figure 5.7
The spike has disappeared.

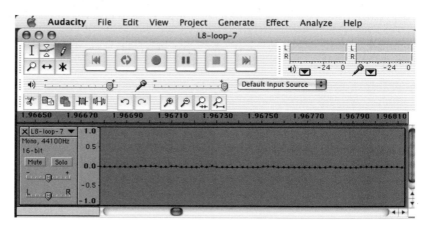

- *Fading up and down* You've found a great loop but you need to fade down the notes near the end. You can do this in GarageBand but it's a tedious procedure (drawing the fade repeatedly using the track volume controls). It's far easier to make a permanent edit in Audacity using a fade effect or drawing one with the envelope tool.

Figure 5.8
Making a permanent edit in Audacity

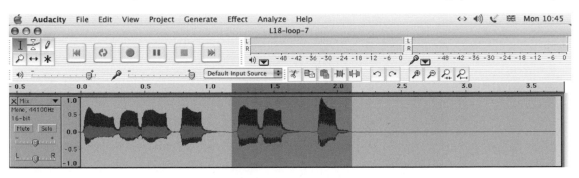

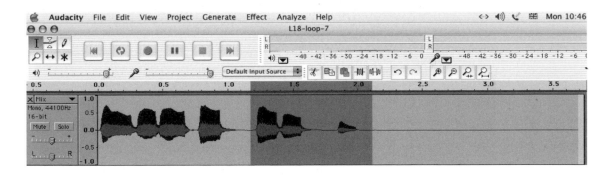

• *Normalizing* You've recorded an audio track that's a bit on the quiet side. You're happy with the take and don't relish the idea of recording it again. How can you raise the overall volume of the track whilst keeping the quietest parts strictly relative to the louder parts? The answer lies, once again, in Audacity. Simply select the audio and apply the normalizing feature.

Figure 5.9
Normalizing is simple in Audacity.

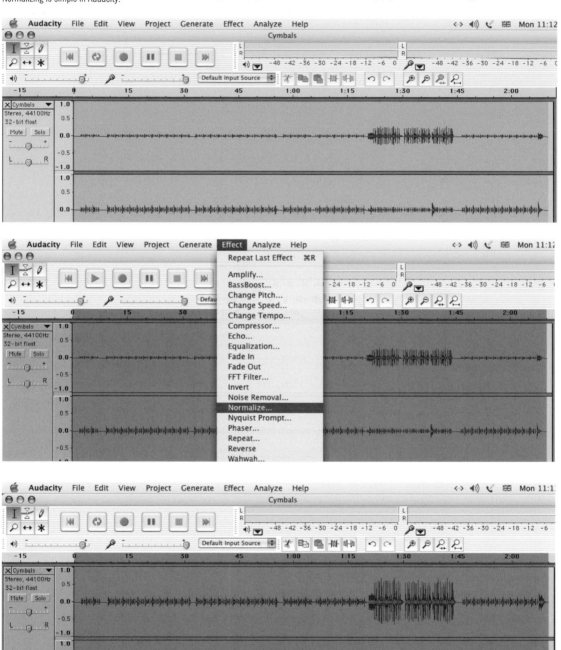

Audacity may not be up to Bias Peak's level but for general audio editing it's a real Swiss Army knife. Some of the other things you can do with it are alter frequencies with equalization, apply compression and use effects like echo, phasing and wah-wah.

Time stretching imported audio files in GarageBand 3

Audio regions that you've recorded yourself (purple) can now be time stretched in GarageBand 2 and 3. But imported audio files (orange) remain immune to GarageBand's time stretching algorithms. You can add them to the loop browser but only as one-shot samples, not as Apple loops. Those crafty old folks at Apple don't want us getting too much for free.

Fortunately the Apple Loops Utility can be brought into play here. You can use it to convert your orange regions into blue regions. In other words transform ordinary audio files into Apple loops. To perform the conversion, follow the instructions in chapter 3, Apple Loops, Home-grown loops. When you're finished simply drag the files back onto the GarageBand timeline and save the song. The new files will show up in the media folder, inside the project file (.band).

Info

Programs like Audacity are called open source software, because their source code is available for anyone to study or use. There are thousands of other free and open source programs, including the Mozilla web browser, the OpenOffice.org office suite, and entire Linux-based operating systems.

MIDI recording

Make it easy on yourself

Playing and recording software instruments takes place on MIDI based tracks (software instrument tracks) and the usual method is to play and record the MIDI data (notes and controller information) using a MIDI keyboard.

MIDI keyboards are like piano keyboards and to play them well requires considerable skill, the same as any other musical instrument. But if your keyboard skills are not up to grade A standard, don't worry. It's a common myth that you have to be a good keyboard player to record MIDI tracks. Many accomplished musicians who play instruments such as guitar and saxophone are terrible piano players but that doesn't prevent them recording MIDI tracks in programs like GarageBand.

Maybe you already play a musical instrument. If so, you must have encountered fast passages that you couldn't play the first time round. What did you do? Give up? Of course not. You practised them slowly. Only when the difficult bits were under-the -fingers did you speed them up again (at least that's what you should have done).

The same principles apply when you're playing a GarageBand software instrument. If you can't play something fast, just slow the tempo, record the part and then return your song to its original tempo. Even if there are still a few wrong notes in there, the beauty of MIDI is that you can always edit your mistakes afterwards.

The GarageBand keyboard

This is the most basic method of playing a software instrument and recording the MIDI data. Press Comand+K to bring it on screen. Just click on the keys with your mouse to play sounds.

Although it works well enough, it's really only good for auditioning the various sounds on offer. Playing a piano style keyboard with a mouse just isn't practical. To play anything half decent you'll need a proper MIDI key-

Figure 6.1
The GarageBand keyboard

board and a MIDI interface of some kind. However, if you don't yet have a MIDI set-up of your own, you can, initially anyway, use GarageBand's on-screen keyboard instead. It's fine for gaining a basic understanding of how GarageBand's software instruments work.

Info

At first glance the GarageBand keyboard appears to be limited to just four octaves. But grab the blue shaded area, above the main keyboard (or the tiny arrows at either end) and move it left or right and you will discover the full range of a real grand piano.

Musical typing

When using the GarageBand keyboard you've probably noticed that you can only play one note at a time. Switching smoothly from one note to another, other than adjacent ones, is difficult to say the least. Another better method for playing software instruments is to use the musical typing feature. Press Shift+Command+K to bring it on screen. This is a hybrid keyboard combining the keys of both a computer keyboard and a conventional piano keyboard.

Now this is very clever because, even if you don't own a MIDI keyboard you can actually play a simple musical line and record it. The keys of a piano keyboard have been mapped to those of a standard computer keyboard. If you've ever played piano, you'll recognise the layout.

Figure 6.2
Press Shift+Command+K to open the musical typing feature.

Real time drums

Using the musical typing keyboard to play and record software instruments isn't going to be everybody's cup of tea, particularly if they are used to playing a piano keyboard. However, if you don't yet own a MIDI keyboard the musical typing facility is a great way to play realistic drums, in real time.

To try it out, create a new GarageBand project and change the default piano track to a rock drum kit (Software Instrument > Drum Kits > Rock Kit), Open the Musical Typing facility. Now practise playing and recording your newly discovered drum kit.

With Octave set to C1 (use keys Z and X to adjust this) the drum kit will be mapped as follows:

A – Kick Drum
S – Snare Drum (tight)
T – Snare Drum (loose)
W – Side Stick
E – Snare Drum Roll
F, G, H, J, K, L – Toms
T – Pedal Hi-hat
Y – Closed Hi-hat
U – Open Hi-hat
O and **:** – Crash Cymbals
P and **'** – Ride Cymbals

Cycle recording

One of the most useful things about recording MIDI in GarageBand is the option to record in a cycle or loop. You can set up a cycle region by pressing the cycle button on the transport controls. You then adjust the start and end points with the yellow ruler that appears beneath the beat ruler. Each time a cycle repeats you can merge new material with any previously recorded data.

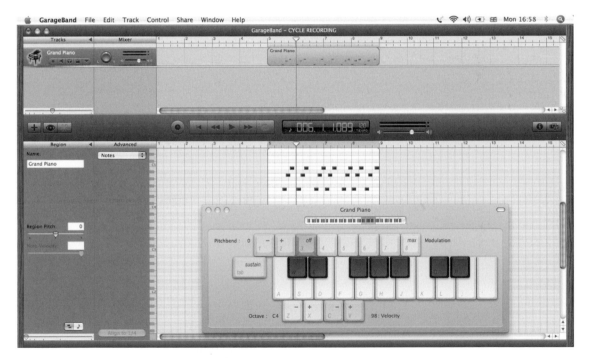

Figure 6.3
Cycle recording – a great way to record in GarageBand.

Recording MIDI based drums using cycle recording

Like all sequencers, GarageBand provides facilities for cycle recording. By setting up a cycle region you can record a region piece by piece, adding something new on each pass. You can do this with all the software instruments but it's probably most useful when compiling a drum track. Here's how it's done:

1 Create a new song. Choose a comfortable speed. Select a grid setting of 1/8 (to begin with). Ensure the count-in is active.
2 Open the Track Info window and change the default Grand Piano track to a drum kit. Choose any kit you fancy.
3 Press the note C1 (Musical Typing: press A) on your MIDI keyboard and you'll hear a kick drum sound. Press E1, two white notes higher (Musical Typing: T), and you'll hear a snare drum.
4 Set up a four bar cycle and record a four-to-the-bar kick drum beat (or something similar). When you reach the end of the cycle, stop playing but leave GarageBand in record mode.
5 As the region cycles you can add snare and hi-hat as and when you like. But keep it simple and use nothing smaller than 1/8 notes (to begin with). Experiment with cymbal crashes and toms as well, if you want. When you're happy, press the spacebar, to stop recording.
6 Play the region back. If it sounds a bit rough, don't worry; just press the Fix Timing (Alighn to 1/8) button in the track editor.

QuickTip

It's okay to stop playing and leave GarageBand in record mode. You'll hear the music you've already recorded; none of it will be erased.

Figure 6.4
Cycle recording drums in GarageBand.

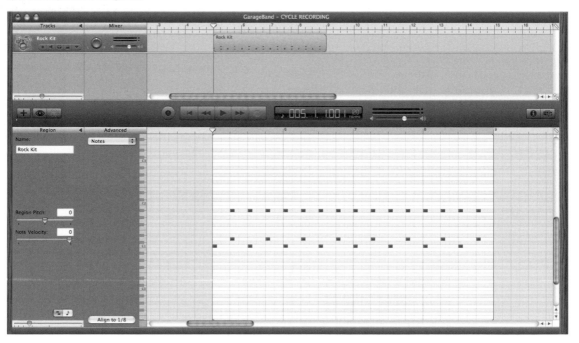

Virtual drumming tips

Here are few pointers when recording 'live style' drums:

- People new to songwriting and sequencing often spend hours perfecting a drum track before they even think about recording anything else. Quite often it has to be scrapped anyway (or at the least, heavily modified), at a later stage, because it doesn't fit the bass part which was influenced by the guitar rhythm, which was influenced by the melody and so on. Often a better bet is to record some melodic material first. Once the melody and bass are down it's much easier to be a 'virtual drummer' and instil spontaneity and feel into the music.
- If possible, record in stretches of eight bars or so at a time. This helps create a natural flow and is preferable to cutting and pasting one or two bar segments.
- Drum rolls are best sequenced manually, using the grid editor. It's no easy matter to roll two fingers as fast as two drum sticks.
- Try playing just the kick and snare drums first and overdub the hi-hats, cymbals and toms afterwards, on separate tracks. Fills can be left until later too. Having the drums separated like this makes it easier to carry out editing procedures.

Get real

If the software instrument you are recording is emulating a real acoustic instrument, forget the keyboard and concentrate on the virtual instrument you are recording. For example, if it's a violin, imagine yourself actually playing it. Become that violinist. The same approach applies to any instrument. Try to get inside the mind of your virtual instrumentalist. Before you can do this confidently, you will almost certainly need to spend time listening to real instruments in the hands of real performers.

Taking control

Use controller data such as pitch bend and modulation to help make software instruments more convincing. It's best done whilst playing, using the controls on your MIDI keyboard. Most MIDI keyboards feature two controller wheels, one for pitch bend, one for modulation, just to the left of the keyboard. The popular M-Audio Keystation 49e is a typical example. You can add controller data afterwards but it's hard to beat the spontaneity of playing live (see Chapter 7, MIDI editing, for controller editing tips).

QuickTip

If you're after realism when sequencing drums, avoid playing three things on the same beat - apart from the kick drum, of course - because drummers don't possess three arms and the result will sound unatural.

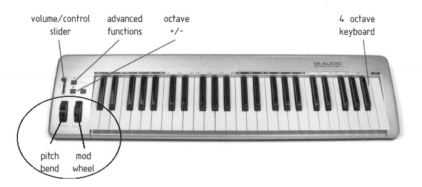

Figure 6.5
The M-Audio Keystaion 49e has two wheels for controlling pitch bend and modulation.

Smoother playing

If you're not too hot on the keyboard your MIDI recordings may sound a bit lumpy due to uneven playing. The keyboard sensitivity slider, found in the Audio/MIDI preferences, can help out here to certain extent. If you're a bit heavy handed and you need to play a gentle passage move the slider to the left. Moving it all the way to the left will prevent you from recording velocities much above the 100 mark.

Figure 6.6
Set the keyboard sensitivity to smooth out uneven playing.

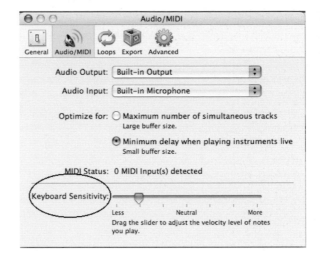

Step by step

Iif you're into step sequencing, useful for making your own dance music patterns, you can enter notes directly into the grid editor. Command-click in a MIDI track (software instrument track) first, to create a region in which to work. You can now enter notes onto the grid with the mouse by Command-clicking (Figure 6.7). 1/8-note appears to be the default length when you add notes this way. To change their duration, just grab the right corner. To change their position, grab the left corner.

If, however, you want to set a new default length for the note(s) you enter, select the notaion view and choose a note value from the drop-down menu (Figure 6.8). Now return to the graphic view and enter the note(s).

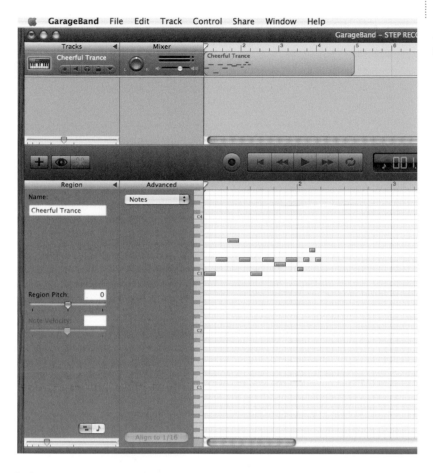

Figure 6.7
Step entry by Command-clicking on the grid.

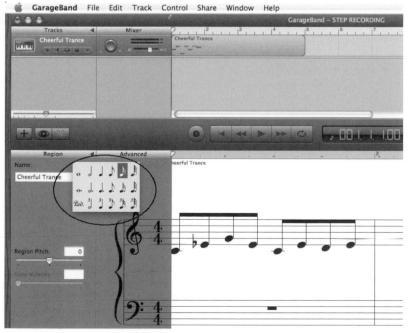

Note by note

If you can read music you can also step enter the notes in the notation editor view. Just Command-click at the points where you want to enter a note. Its duration value can be determined using the drop-down menu, just to the left of the staff. To lengthen a note, grab its right corner and drag.

Echo your tracks

Try adding echo to your MIDI parts as you play. You can switch it on and adjust the level in the track info window. You'll soon notice that the repeats are synchronised with the song tempo. Having the echo switched on will influence how you perform the music, probably forcing you to reduce the amount of notes you play. This is no bad thing for certain types of music, particularly in the reggae and dub genres.

Figure 6.9
Adjust echo parameters with the sliders.

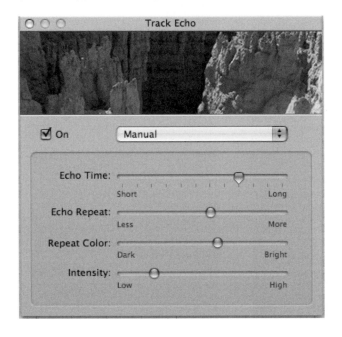

MIDI editing

Smooth things over

When emulating monophonic instruments (those that play one note at a time, such as trumpets and saxophones) whilst playing a keyboard be careful not to create overlaps. It's easily done. Check the notes afterwards in the editor. If you find any, shorten them so that they line up adjacently to each other. This will make the performance sound more natural.

Figure 7.1
Overlapping notes (top pic) sound unnatural, so adjust note lengths to suit the instrument being emulated (bottom pic).

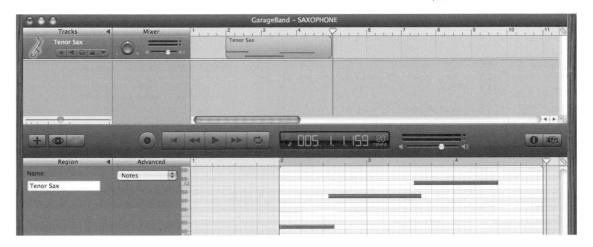

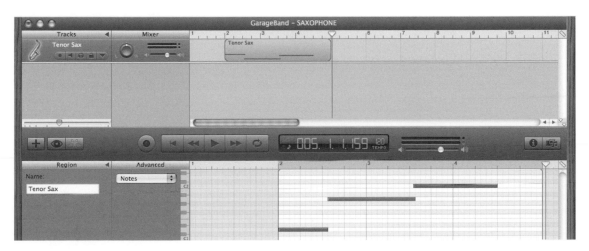

Info

Monophonic linstruments are restricted to sounding just one note at a time. Two typical examples are the trumpet and saxophone. Polyphonic instruments can sound more than one note at a time. Two typical examples are the piano and guitar.

Figure 7.2
For instruments like strings, create small note overlaps in the grid editor.

QuickTip

For making fine adjustments to note lengths and positions in the editor, move the zoom slider (lower left corner) to the right. Grid resolutions of 1/32 and 1/64 are best for small adjustments. The timeline grid must be set to Automatic for the zoom function to work.

Mind the gap

Sometimes overlapping notes are just what's needed. To smooth things out after playing a long flowing line (strings maybe), check the recorded notes in the grid editor. Create small note overlaps for a legato effect. For best results, change the grid setting in the editor to 1/32 or 1/64. This will allow you to make very small adjustments to note lengths.

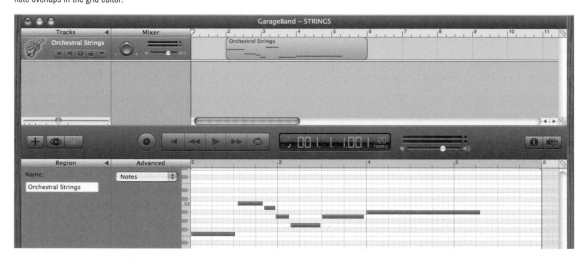

Editing controller data

After you've recorded a part with, let's say, pitchbend added (see page 55, Taking Control, for details) you can edit the data. Select the recently played region and then, in the editor (advanced section), select Pitchbend from the drop-down menu. You will now see the pitch bend controller information displayed as nodes and lines on the grid. Drag the control-points around with your mouse. If you want to draw new ones, press Command - a pencil tool appears.

Five types of MIDI controller can be recorded, edited and drawn in GarageBand:

Modulation

Often used on strings and woodwinds to simulate vibrato. Go easy though, to avoid that 'nanny goat' sound.

Modulation data is displayed on the grid as an envelope and represented numerically. The higher the value, the more intense the effect.

Figure 7.3
Modulation data represented as a graph.

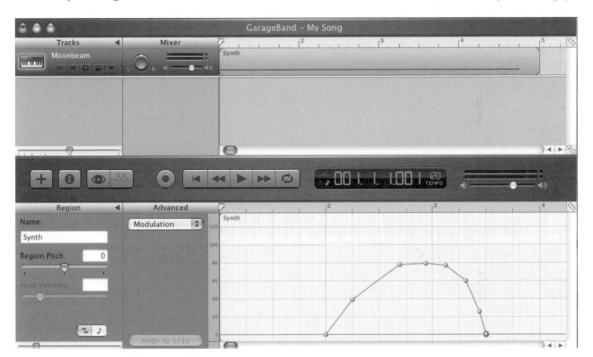

Pitchbend

Often used to simulate note bending, as used on guitar and wind instruments. Use sparingly. However, feel free to let rip on wild synthesizer lead patches.

Pitchbend data is displayed on the grid as an envelope. Anything above zero raises the pitch. Anything below zero lowers the pitch. You can alter the curve by selecting and dragging the control-points.

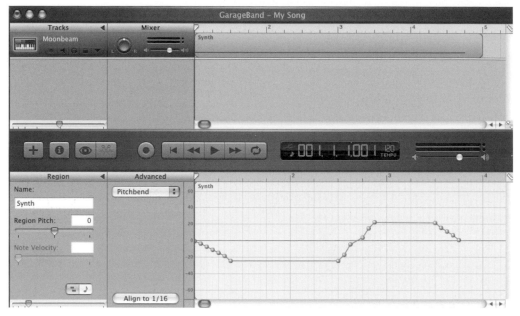

Figure 7.4
Pitchbend data.

Figure 7.5
Sustain data. Sustain is turned on in bar 1 and is turned off at bar 2.

Sustain

This has the same effect as holding down a piano's sustain pedal - the notes ring on. If you don't have a sustain pedal with your MIDI keyboard it's easy to draw the on/off data with a mouse. Sustain is simply switched on or off. In the picture below, sustain is turned on in bar 1 and is turned off at bar 2.

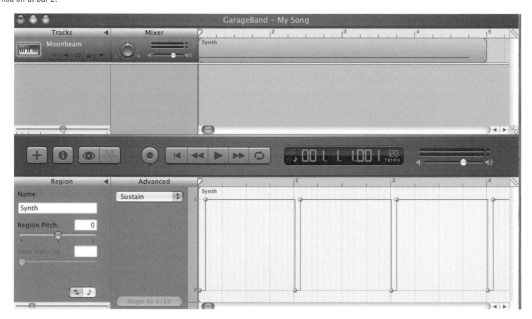

Expression

This is a very useful controller, used in exactly the same way as volume. But whereas volume control is mainly used to control the entire track, expression can be used within a region, to control individual note volume.

Expression data is displayed on the grid as an envelope and represented numerically. The higher the value, the more intense the effect.

Figure 7.6
Expression data.

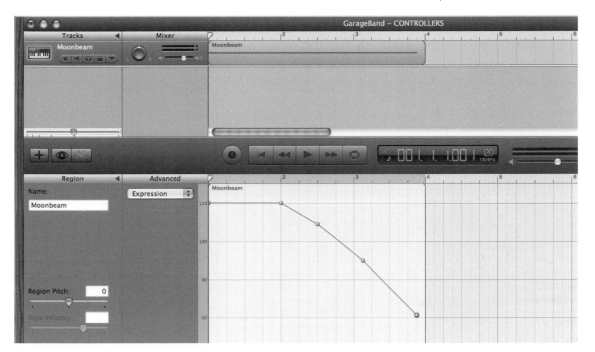

Foot control

Many of the instruments supplied in Apple's Jam Packs support a wide variety of articulations. This controller can be used to access them.

Foot Control data is displayed on the grid as an envelope and represented numerically. The higher the value, the more intense the effect.

QuickTip

For precisely spaced auto panning and controller zig-zags make sure Automatic is selected when you choose a timeline grid setting.

Controller effects tricks

If you're into dance music and electronica you can use the controllers in GarageBand to create many of the effects you hear on your favourite tracks.

- Gating effect – this works well on synth like GarageBand's Koto Chords. Record a note for a bar or two and enter zig-zag style expression controller points into the grid editor at regular spaces. This one uses alternate values of 120 and 0.
- Panning effect – you can achieve the classic auto-panning effect using Track Pan. Just enter zig-zag style control-points along the time-line grid.

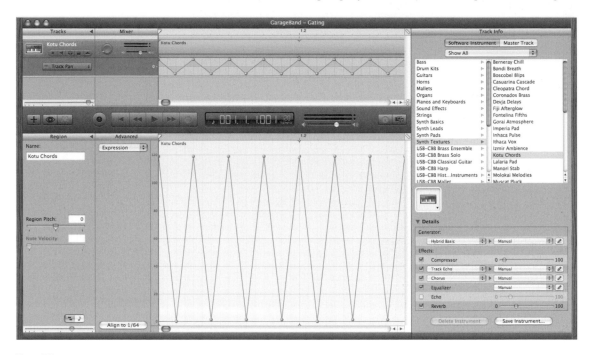

Figure 7.7
Gating and panning.

QuickTip

When drawing in controller data, for greater accuracy, enlarge the editor (see Chapter 2, Working methods, Big Ed, for details) and use the slider to increase the grid resolution.

Velocity editing

Using the keyboad velocity slider in the Audio/MIDI preferences will help you adjust the velocity level of notes as you play. Even so, some velocities will probably need tweaking after recording. Unfortunately you'll have to do this manually, one note at a time. Simply select a note on the grid editor and reduce or increase its velocity value with the slider.

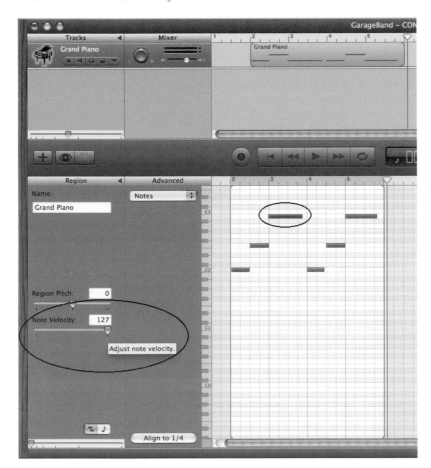

Figure 7.8
Editing velocity values manually.

Drum kit combinations

Apple have followed the GM standard for mapping most of their drum kit sounds to a piano keyboard. This is very convenient because it means you can combine different drum kits to play a drum loop. Here's how it's done:

1   Locate and drag the loop called Classic Rock Beat 03 onto the timeline.

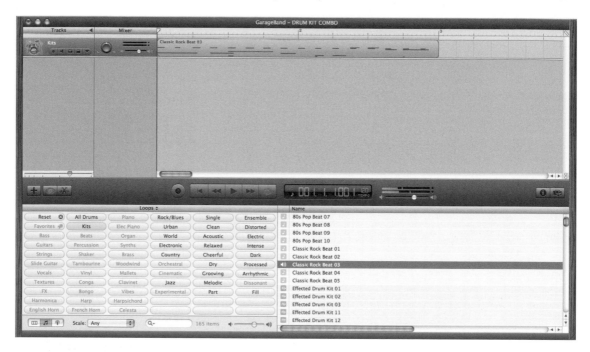

2   Repeat the process to create an identical region directly below the first one. Assign the first track to a Rock kit and the second to a Hip Hop kit.

3   Delete all the hi-hats (F#1 and G#1) and toms (A1, G1 and F1) on track one (the rock kit).

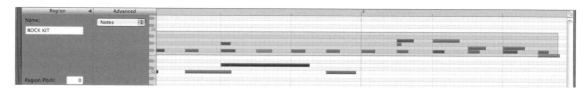

4 Delete the kick drum (C1) and snare drum (D1) on track two (the hip hop kit).

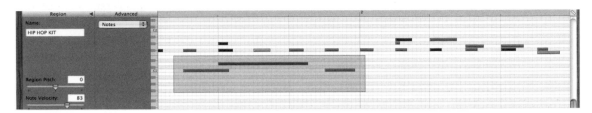

By combining the two kits you have created a single hybrid kit. You could take this a stage further by creating a third track and deleting all the sounds except the snare drum. With the snare drum now assigned to its own track you are free to apply further processing without affecting the other sounds (don't forget to delete the snare drum on track two).

If you take this process to its logical conclusion you can assign every drum sound within a kit to individual MIDI tracks. This will give you total control over volume, panning and processing for each drum sound.

GM drums

Apple loops conform to the GM standard drum map most of the time. Editing them and creating hybrid kits is much easier if you are familiar with the layout.

35	B0	Acoustic Bass Drum	59	B2	Ride Cymbal 2
36	C1	Bass Drum 1	60	C3	Hi Bongo
37	C#1	Side Stick	61	C#3	Low Bongo
38	D1	Acoustic Snare	62	D3	Mute Hi Conga
39	D#1	Hand Clap	63	D#3	Open Hi Conga
40	E 1	Electric Snare	64	E3	Low Conga
41	F1	Low Floor Tom	65	F3	High Timbale
42	F#1	Closed Hi-Hat	66	F#3	Low Timbale
43	G1	High Floor Tom	67	G3	High Agogo
44	G#1	Pedal Hi-Hat	68	G#3	Low Agogo
45	A1	Low Tom	69	A3	Cabasa
46	A#1	Open Hi-Hat	70	A#3	Maracas
47	B1	Low-Mid Tom	71	B3	Short Whistle
48	C2	Hi-Mid Tom	72	C4	Long Whistle
49	C#2	Crash Cymbal 1	73	C#4	Short Guiro
50	D2	High Tom	74	D4	Long Guiro
51	D#2	Ride Cymbal 1	75	D#4	Claves
52	E2	Cymbal	76	E4	Hi Wood Block
53	F2	Ride Bell	77	F4	Low Wood Block
54	F#2	Tambourine	78	F#4	Mute Cuica
55	G2	Splash Cymbal	79	G4	Open Cuica
56	G#2	Cowbell	80	G#4	Mute Triangle
57	A2	Crash Cymbal 2	81	A4	Open Triangle
58	A#2	Vibraslap			

Info

GM stands for General MIDI. This is a set of requirements for MIDI devices and software aimed at ensuring consistent playback performance on all instruments.

QuickTip

You can spice up a dull drum loop by drawing in fills and variations in the grid editor.

The human touch

All good sequencers include MIDI quantisation facilities and GarageBand is no exception, although it is somewhat limited. Apple have called it Fix Timing. You can use it to correct any timing mistakes you might have made whilst recording. The notes will be snapped to the grid resolution of your choice, 1/8, 1/16 and so on. The only problem is that everything will be hard quantised, without any humanisation qualities.

But what if you want to correct only those notes that have strayed out of time, without destoying the natural human feel of the other notes? It can be done but the process is a little tedious. After recording, select only the notes that you need to correct, either in groups or one at a time. Click on the ruler in the top right corner of the grid editor to select the appropriate quantisation setting. Press the 'Align to' button to quantise the notes.

The notes in this screenshot are slightly out of time and selected for quantisation.

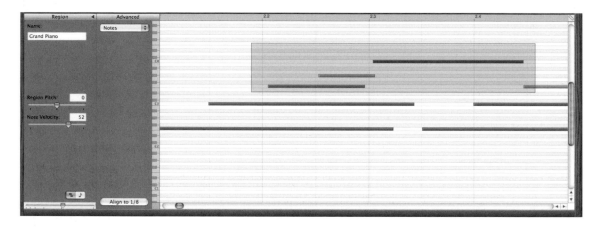

After aligning them to a grid reference of 1/32, the selected notes are now sounding in time.

If it ain't got that swing...

The Fix Timing feature can be used creatively, to inject swing into Apple loops. For example, load the Apple loop called Classic Rock Beat 03, select all the notes in the grid editor and apply 1/8 Swing Heavy quantisation. This is a great way to completely transform the character of many standard GarageBand Apple loops.

Figure 7.9
Classic Rock Beat 03 before quantisation.

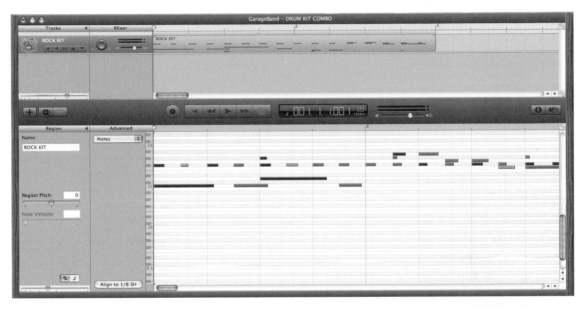

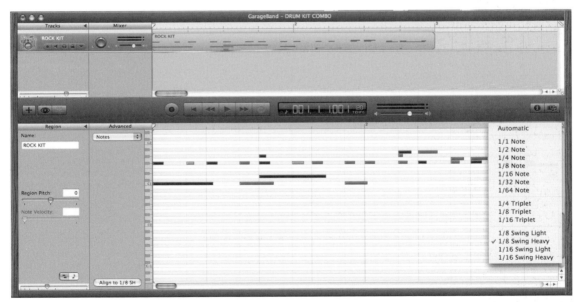

Figure 7.10
Classic Rock Beat 03 after 1/8 Swing Heavy quantisation. Note the effect on the kick drum and hi-hat cymbal.

Transposing regions

A common problem: You've recorded, let's say, 12 bars of music onto a MIDI track and there's a four bar section in the middle that you would like to transpose. But the region pitch slider in the editor transposes the whole track. What do you do? The solution is easy. With the split command, make the four bars you need to transpose into an individual region. Now select it and use the region pitch slider to alter the pitch of the notes.

Figure 7.11
Split the track into different regions to tranpose just one section of music.

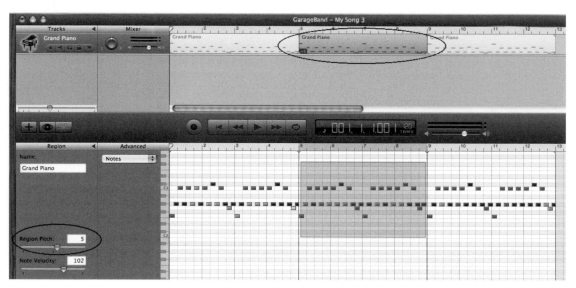

Software instruments

The software instruments in GarageBand are superb and using them is a breeze with the aid of descriptive presets. However, although the online help tells you how to record a software instrument and choose a few sounds, it doesn't tell you that these are the same powerful synthesizers as those found in Logic Pro, only with simplified controls. Once you discover their true potential, there are some powerful editing features just begging to be used. Here's a list of the different types:

Sample-based instruments

Based on Logic Pro's super sampler, the EXS24, these instruments feature sampled recordings of real acoustic instruments, such as violins, drums and percussion, woodwinds, grand pianos and so on. Use them when you need to create realistic interpretations of real acoustic instruments and ensembles.

Analogue-style synthesizers

Based on Logic Pro's brilliant ES2 soft-synth. Instruments in this category include the Analog Basic, Analog Mono, Analog Pad, Analog Swirl and Analog Sync. Use these for all your classic vintage synth sounds (ideal for dance and techno music).

Digital synthesizers

Also based on the ES2, these instruments are optimised to reproduce the classic sounds of instruments like the Yamaha DX7 and Korg M1 both of which feature FM and wavetable synthesis. You can choose between Digital Basic, Digital Mono and the Digital Stepper. Use these instruments when you want that bright, hard-edged sound associated with the synths of the 1980s.

Physically modelled synthesizers

Based on Logic Pro's EVB3, EVP88 and EVD6. These three instruments provide fantastically realistic emulations of the soulful sounding Hammond B3 Organ, the funky Hohner Clavinet and the groovy Fender Rhodes and Wurlitzer electric pianos. The GarageBand equivalents are named Tonewheel Organ, Electric Clavinet and Electric Piano respectively. Use them whenever you want to conjure up authentic jazz, rock and blues keyboard sounds in your productions.

Hybrid synthesizers

Hybrid Basic and Hybrid Morph. These two fantastic instruments actually appeared in GarageBand before they did in Logic Pro. Both are sample-based and produce sounds reminiscent of the classic Korg Wavestation. Use them whenever you need big swirling synth pads, choirs and extraordinary spacey sounds.

Take it away

To make the most of these software instruments and go beyond the presets, you'll need to edit them. And to do that, you'll need a basic knowledge of how synthesizers work.

Most of the GarageBand software instruments produce their sounds using subtractive synthesis. It's a three-stage process: Oscillator > Filter > Amplifier.

Generation

An oscillator is used to produce a harmonically rich sound (an audio signal). The full-scale Logic Pro versions allow you to choose a waveform – sine, square, triangle and so on. However, the GarageBand versions have a fixed waveform optimised for the individual instruments. The exceptions to this rule are the Hybrid synths, which allow you to choose a predetermined waveform type from a drop-down menu.

Sound shaping

Certain frequencies are removed from the sound by passing it through a filter. Most of GarageBand's synthesizers use 'lowpass' filtering – sounds above a set frequency are reduced in volume and sounds below it are allowed to pass through unaffected. A simple low to high cutoff slider is used to control the filter. Some of the GarageBand generators include a resonance slider, used to boost volume at the filter cutoff frequency. Synthesizers with this feature each have their own characteristic resonance. Using the slider will bring the resonance to the fore, more readily defining their signature sound.

Amplification

Controls that determine the sound's volume over the duration of a single note. The editable parameters are:

- Attack – how long it takes the sound to begin immediately after the key is pressed; fast, short attack times for percussive-like sounds such as picked bass and slow, long durations for legato sounds like bowed strings.
- Decay – how long it takes the sound to fall from the peak attack time to the sustain level. Percussive sounds like drums have fast decay times, no matter how long you hold down the key. A plucked string sound will take longer decay if the key is held down.
- Sustain – the volume of sound, once the decay has ended with the key held down.
- Release – how long it takes the sound to die away immediately after the key is released.

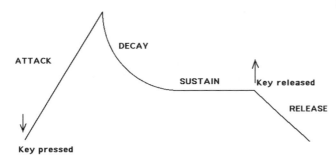

Figure 8.1
ADSR. Attack, decay, sustain and release.

As mentioned above, the GarageBand instruments are cut-down versions of the very much larger EXS24 and ES2 Logic Pro instruments. As such, many of them are limited to just a few editable parameters. Fortunately, Apple have thought carefully about which parameters to leave in place and which ones to discard for each instrument. What follows is a closer look at each type of software instrument and their parameter controls.

Info

Attack, decay, sustain and release times are commonly referred to as ADSR in synthesizer parlance.

Sample-based instruments

All the acoustic instruments here feature cutoff frequency and release controls. The horns, strings and voice samples have additional attack controls.

- Use the cutoff frequency slider to soften an instrument's tone and mute its higher frequencies. In other words, make it mellower.
- Use the release controls to tailor the guitar and piano sounds. A fast release (slider to the left) is useful when you want a dampened effect. To lend a natural ring to the strings move the slider to the right, gradually introducing a slower release time.
- For loud horn parts use a short attack time. For mellower legato passages reduce the attack time. The same goes for strings but in general, a slower attack time will be the norm.
- For woodwinds and saxes, a medium to fast attack time will fit most situations.

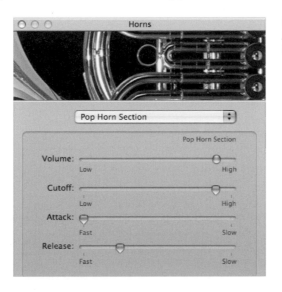

Figure 8.2
Adjusting the characteristics of sampled instruments in GarageBand.

Analogue-style synthesizers

Based on the Logic Pro ES2, different parameters are dished up for the various instrument versions. Sometimes these parameters are labelled in confusing Apple-speak terms such as 'richness' (a slider that tunes the oscillators in the Analog Mono synthesizer). Nevertheless, despite being technically unorthodox, the names are fairly apt descriptions of the resulting sounds.

Analog Basic

A good all-rounder, this one, and great for all those typical analogue-style basses, leads and pads used in today's dance and techno music. Warm in character, it benefits greatly from a touch of chorus, which can be easily added in the Details section of the track info window.

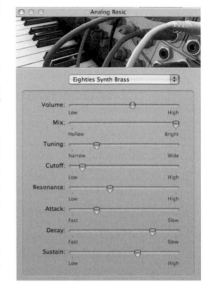

Editable parameters here include cutoff, resonance, attack, decay and sustain. Only the release parameter is missing but a touch of echo or reverb will provide a tail to the sound, if that's what you're after.

This synth employs two oscillators, a square wave (Hollow) and a sawtooth wave (Bright). Use the 'mix' slider to blend them together.

The tuning slider is used to vary the amount of detuning between the two oscillators. At the fully left (Narrow) position and for a short distance to the right you'll hear the two oscillators finely tuned in unison. As you move the slider to the right the tuning between the two oscillators gradually becomes coarser. About halfway across the two oscillators sound firstly as fifths, then as octaves and double octaves.

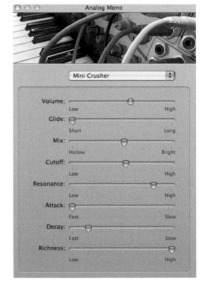

Analog Mono

As the name implies, this is a mono synthesizer; it can only sound one note at a time. Editable parameters here include glide, mix, cutoff, resonance, attack, decay and richness.

The main difference between this instrument and the Analog Basic is the lack of a sustain control. Hold down a note and it will sound until you release the key. Sustain, therefore, is always on.

Another big difference is the addition of a Glide control, known in synth-speak as portamento. Play one note immediately after another (with a slight overlap) and you'll hear the first note slide up to the second note. The further to the right that you move the slider, the longer the glide takes to reach its destination. Use it for special effects. However for general playing a modest setting is best.

The Richness slider, at the bottom, is used to vary the amount of detuning between the two oscillators (very similar to the Tuning slider in the Analog Basic).

Analog Pad

Editable parameters on this synthesizer include modulation, character, cutoff, resonance, cutoff envelope, duration and animation.

The key to the instrument's rich pad sounds is the Modulation control, used to modulate the main oscillator, a rectangular shaped pulse wave. To illustrate this, load the Analog Dreams preset, hold a long note (not too high a note, you'll see why in a moment) and reduce the modulation. Doing so will thin the sound considerably. Move it back to the right and that rich chorus type quality returns. Move the slider to the far right and the richness is even more intensified.

Continue holding the note and move the Character slider to the right. You'll notice that the bass frequencies are gradually removed from the note, indicating the presence of a highpass filter. There is more going on here, behind the scenes, but if you use it as a highpass filter, you'll not go far wrong.

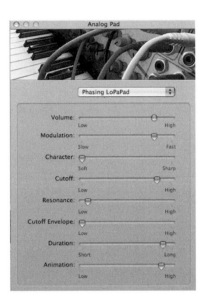

The Duration slider appears to combine attack, decay, sustain and release in a single control. The far left position provides fast attack and release times. Move the slider to the right for slower attack and release times – a little crude perhaps but fine for pad sounds.

The oddly named Animation slider introduces a phasing effect whilst simultaneously panning the sound in the stereo picture. Load the preset named Phasing LoPaPad for a glorious example.

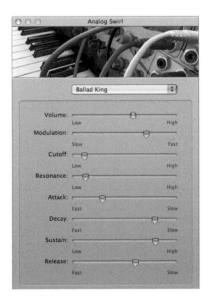

Analog Swirl

Editable parameters here include modulation, cutoff, resonance, attack, decay, sustain and release; all in all, a conventionally named set of controls.

As with the Analog Pad, a Modulation slider is in evidence. And like that instrument, pulse-width modulation is the name of the game. The modulated sound is passed through the usual cutoff filters and on to the ADSR envelopes.

It's a versatile synth with an edgy sound and capable of a variety of powerful trance-style leads as well as percussive arpeggios. The presets bear this out.

Analog Sync

Editable parameters here are sync, sync modulation, sync envelope, cut-off, attack, decay and sustain.

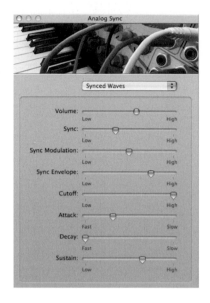

In this synthesizer three oscillators are firstly, synchronised and then two of them are gradually detuned in relationship to the main oscillator. To find out how this works, play a long note with the three Sync controls in their 'low' position (all sliders left). Now move the Sync slider gradually to the right and you'll hear the different tunings. Note how most of the time the main, deeper sounding oscillator remains constant (it occasionally disappears altogether).

Moving the Modulation slider gradually to the right imparts motion to the sound, which in the far right position produces an intense, cyclic propeller like sound. The Envelope slider can be used to further intensify the effect.

The Groovy Sync and Synced Waves presets are both good examples of the synchronisation features in action.

As well as its normal duties, the Attack slider introduces a volume fade-up, when set to slow attack times. Slow attack times also produce slow release times as well – strange but true.

Digital-style synthesizers

Like the analogue-style synths, these instruments are derived from Logic Pro's ES2. But this time, wavetable and FM sounds are used in conjunction with traditional synthesis techniques.

Digital Basic

This synth uses frequency modulation (FM) to create complex audio waveforms used for creating bell sounds, soft pads and even synthesised percussion. Editable parameters include mix, tuning, harmonics, timbre, attack, decay and release.

The Mix slider is used to vary the signal between the Modulated (left) and Direct (right) signals. The Tuning slider alters a note's pitch in semi-tone steps between Low and High. The Harmonics slider is used to select digital waveforms, of which there are many. The Timbre slider alters the tone.

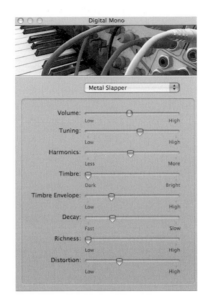

Digital Mono

Sliders here include tuning, harmonics, timbre, timbre envelope, decay, richness, and distortion. As the name implies, only single notes can be played on this instrument. It's similar to the Digital Basic but you'll notice that it lacks the Mix slider. That's because there is no direct FM signal output, just a modulated one.

The Timbre slider controls the overall modulation. The Timbre Envelope changes the sound from abrasive to mellow sounds – load the Sine Bass preset and move the slider to the Bright (right) position to see what I mean. The Richness slider detunes the oscillator and fattens the sounds.

You'll find it difficult to produce pretty noises with this instrument but it's great for nasty sounding basses.

Digital Stepper

Editable controls here include balance, modulation, harmonics, harmonic steps, cutoff, cutoff steps and duration.

This synthesizer combines analogue-type and digital-type synthesis. It's called Stepper, presumably, because it's capable of producing

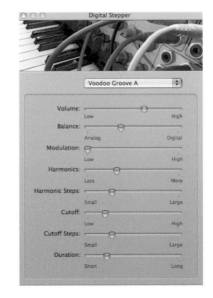

rhythmic, randomised harmonic steps when notes are held.

The Harmonics slider works the same as in the Digital Basic and is used for selecting one of the many digital waveforms available. The Balance slider is used to bring either the analogue-type sounds or the digital-type sounds to prominence. A chorus effect can be introduced with the Modulation slider (oscillator detuning).

The Harmonic Steps slider is used to control the randomised harmonic steps, mentioned above. To increase the range of the steps, move the slider towards 'more'. Load the Voodoo Groove preset to see how it works. The Cutoff Steps parameter introduces randomised frequency cutoff. The Duration slider works like a release control.

As you've probably gathered by now, this synthesizer is perfect for producing rich pulsating pads for trance music.

Physically modelled synths

GarageBand has three physically modelled synthesizers, which are based on Logic Pro's EVB3, EVP88 and EVD6. These three instruments provide fantastically realistic emulations of the soulful sounding Hammond B3 Organ, the funky Hohner Clavinet and the groovy Fender Rhodes and Wurlitzer electric pianos. Despite being cut-down versions, these instruments are truly superb.

Electric Clav

Oh yes, I like this one! Only one slider here, apart from the volume control, which makes it easy to use and great fun to play. The Damper slider emulates the string muting of a real clavinet. In the High position the strings are fully dampened. In the Low position the sound is much more edgy and bright.

This instrument will benefit greatly from added effects. Chorus smoothes out the sound nicely, for background chord work. Auto Wah coupled with the Phaser provides a talking-type effect, superb for funky riffs.

Electric Piano

The Fender Rhodes and Wurlitzer pianos are absolute classics and this instrument provides great emulations of both types. Like the Electric Clav, with just a single fader control and two mode buttons, it's a cinch to use. The Tines model provides the Rhodes sounds. The Reeds model provides the Wurly sounds.

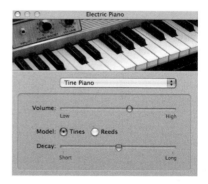

> **QuickTip**
>
> To increase the stereo panning of the steps produced by Digital Stepper, move either the Harmonic Steps or the Cutoff Steps sliders to the right.

> **QuickTip**
>
> The Electric Clav is perfect for funky Stevie Wonder style riffs. Remember 'Superstition'. Use the Auto Wah and Phaser effects to spice it up.

> **QuickTip**
>
> Choose the Reeds mode on the Electric Piano for percussive woody sounding keyboard sounds - think 'Dreamer' by Supertramp.

> **QuickTip**
>
> Choose the Tines mode on the Electric Piano for mellow jazzy keyboard sounds - think 'You Are The Sunshine Of My Life' by Stevie Wonder.

Tonewheel Organ

Aha, that famous Hammond sound. Parameters available here are drawbars, percussion level, percussion time, click, distortion and three speaker types.

The Drawbar slider contains a set of useful preset drawbar combinations. Towards the Less position the sounds are distinctly church-like; loading the Cathedral presets will bear this out. Towards the More position the sounds are brighter; load the Simple Organ, to see what I mean.

The Percussion Level slider is used to add punch to a note's attack at either the second (left) or third (right) harmonic. The Percussion Time slider provides the decay. The distinctive 'click' of the B-3 Hammond can be adjusted using the Click slider.

Three different Leslie cabinet emulations can be selected at the bottom of the interface – Chorale, Brake and Tremolo and distortion can also be added using the – yes, you've guessed it – the Distortion slider.

Hybrid synthesizers

Two new synthesizers, the Hybrid Basic and the Hybrid Morph found their way into GarageBand 2. Both are sample-based and, apart from the usual editable parameters such as ADSR plus cutoff and resonance controls, they are limited to a few powerful, but easy to use parameters.

Both feature Waveform pop-up menus, for selecting a predetermined sample set. These are used to generate the basic sounds. In the case of the Hybrid Morph, each waveform is actually based on two sample layers and The Morph slider is used to control the crossfades between them. The Morph Envelope slider is used to control the morph over time. To see how it works try this:

1 Select the Analog Blend preset.
The Morph parameter is set to A.
The Morph Envelope is in the 'Off' position.

QuickTip

Both the Wurlitzer and the Rhodes sounds of the Electric Piano will benefit from liberal use of effects such as auto wah, phasing and chorus.

QuickTip

You can switch between the 'chorale' and 'tremolo' rotary speaker settings using a sustain pedal, if your keyboard controller supports it.

2 Play a long note and you'll hear a bright sounding, sawtooth waveform (A).

3 Now move the Morph Envelope slider about halfway towards the B to A setting. Play the note again and you will now hear a second waveform (B), sounding an octave lower, mixed in with the first waveform (A). But there's no morphing going on, just the two waveforms sounding together. That's because the morphing takes place in accordance with the ADSR envelope settings.

4 Now move the Sustain slider some way to the left and play the note again. Aha! Let the morphing commence. Waveform B now morphs smoothly into waveform B.

If you set the Morph parameter to A and the Morph Envelope to From A to B (or vice versa) sometimes, again according to the ADSR settings, you'll hear not hear waveform B, or very little of it anyway. For example, try this:

5 Select the Bell Noise preset. The Morph parameter is set to A. The Morph Envelope slider is set to From B to A.

6 Move the Morph Envelope slider all the way left to the 'From A to B' position.

7 Play a note now and you'll hear just the waveform A.

8 Play the note again and gradually introduce waveform B using the modulation wheel on your keyboard.

In the Hybrid Basic synthesizer you can use the Wheel to Vibrato and Wheel to Cutoff sliders to determine which parameters the modulation wheel controls. This is very useful if you want to create long filter build-ups so often heard on trance recordings.

Both of these professional sounding synths are capable of some very spectacular sounds indeed and certainly put paid to any notion that GarageBand should be considered a toy. Spend time experimenting with them and I'm sure you'll agree. Watch it though they're addictive.

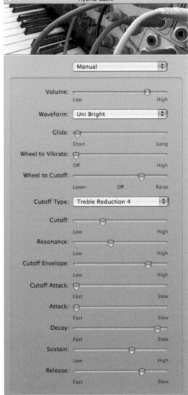

All in order

The effects on a GarageBand audio track follow a fixed order. Gate, Compressor and Equaliser are permanently available and simply turned on and off. In between the compressor and the equalizer there are two blank slots where you can select other GarageBand effects plus any third party Audio Unit processors installed on your Mac. All five effects are known as 'insert effects' and are track specific.

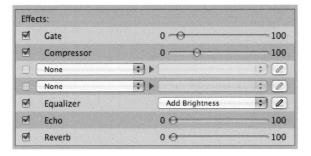

The last two slots, Echo and Reverb, are known as 'send effects'. Their parameters are set in the Master track but their send levels are determined here, on a track-by-track basis.

The available effects on a MIDI track are identical except for the omission of the noisegate.

And how do you use these effects? Basically, however you like. Anything goes, as long as it works. Having said that, general rules of thumb and audio engineering conventions do exist. To begin with at least, you'd be wise to follow them. Here's a rundown of the effects available in GarageBand and a few pointers on how to use them.

Gate

A noise gate (sometimes called an expander) removes unwanted noises during gaps in the audio. When the input level falls below a predetermined threshold, the gate reduces the gain. In other words, when a track's voice or instrument stops playing for a moment, the gate kicks in and turns down the volume. Any noise you or your instrument might have made when you ceased singing or playing – rustling lyric sheets, guitar hums and crackles, foot-tapping, knocking over the microphone stand (only joking), even breathing – can be removed during the pause.

Compressor

A compressor works as an automatic volume control, turning down the volume when the audio is too loud and turning it up when it's too quiet. Why should you need that?

Suppose you've recorded a vocal and, on listening back, you discover that your voice varied considerably in volume over the course of the song. The high notes were sung more vigorously and as a result, were recorded louder. They tend to leap out of the mix. The lower notes were sung with less intensity and the recorded signal is rather low. They tend to get buried in the mix. You could, of course, ride the faders (constantly adjust them while you're mixing), to obtain an even signal. But that's a difficult task even on a hardware console, let alone using a mouse in GarageBand. You could also set up an automated volume curve but finding and rectifying all the uneven spots is a time consuming task.

A compressor does all this for you, automatically. When the input level exceeds a predetermined threshold the compressor reduces the gain. When the input signal is below the threshold, it's unaffected.

Compression can also be used creatively, to beef up guitar, bass and drums in rock music. Dance music producers also use heavy doses of compression on bass and drums, to get that floor-quaking effect.

GarageBand's compressor is very simple to operate. Just use the slider to increase the compression effect.

Equalizer

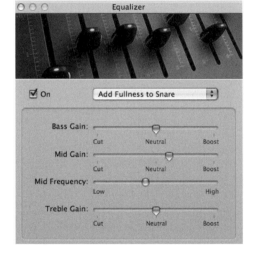

Equalisation (EQ) is a fancy term for tone control. You use it in the same way that you use the treble and bass controls on the average hi-fi unit. But in GarageBand you use it on a track-by-track basis to balance the high, low and midrange frequencies of individual instruments and vocals. To get started, choose a preset from the pop-up menu.

You can cut or boost bass and treble frequencies using a single slider. The midrange frequencies are adjustable. Using a second slider, you firstly select a specific frequency, between the lows and highs, before cutting and boosting the signal in the normal way.

Bass and treble reduction

These two effects are extremely useful when mixing. Technically speaking they're known as lowpass and highpass filters. In other words they're used to let certain frequencies through while rejecting others. The bass reduction tool (lowpass filter) cuts frequencies above a specified point, determined with the slider. Use it to reduce muddiness at the low end of your mixes, often caused by two sounds competing for the same frequencies, bass and drums perhaps. In a dance track it might even be two drum loops that are competing for space.

Vocals too can suffer from booming, as a result of the singer moving in too close to the microphone. Rather than repeat what might otherwise be a great take, use the bass reduction tool to shave the enhanced bass frequencies (known as the proximity effect).

QuickTip

On lead vocals and acoustic instruments, use the compression slider sparingly, adding just enough to make the vocal sit nicely in the mix. Too much compression can spoil an otherwise exciting performance.

QuickTip

Try to use EQ correctively, to bring out a particular element (a vocal perhaps) of a recording that might otherwise be buried in the mix.

QuickTip

Cutting a frequency is usually better than trying to boost it. You want to hear more highs? Try cutting the lows first (before boosting the highs).

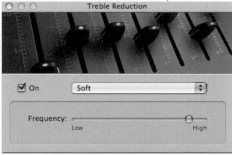

The treble reduction tool works in the same way but cuts frequencies below the specified frequency.

Distortion and Overdrive

These are guitar-derived effects. If you need to crunch-up your guitar, or anything else for that matter, you can use these tools to do it. Distortion will provide you with the sound of wrecked speakers (without the expense of actually ruining your

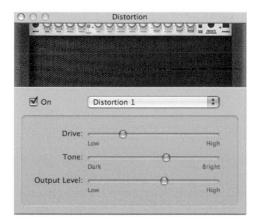
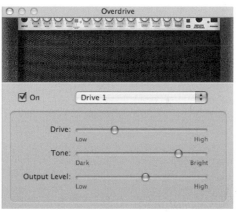

amp) and Overdrive will provide a similar effect but warmer and more musical. Apart from guitar, try them out on drum loops for a nasty industrial effect.

Bitcrusher

A cut down version of Logic Pro's ultimate distortion box, this one's for people who like their music on the nasty side. The resolution slider progressively destroys the pristine 16-bit audio you painstakingly recorded onto your hard-drive. Take it to the limit and hear for yourself! The second slider is used to resample the audio in real time. Again an effect that's rather difficult to put into mere words. Use it to crunch-up synths, guitars and whatever else takes your fancy.

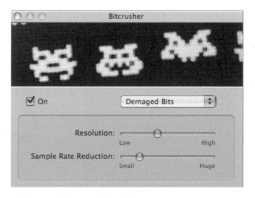

Automatic Filter

Like Bitcrusher, this one's derived from Logic Pro. And like the bass reduction tool, mentioned earlier, it's a lowpass filter but with a couple of extra features. You use the frequency slider to determine the point where the filter kicks in and the resonance slider to emphasise the frequency range at the cut-off point. As you increase the resonance, the filter oscillates.

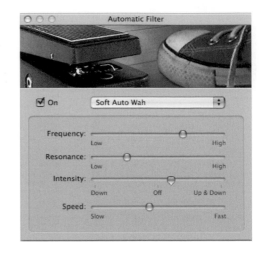

Another warning: don't move it too far otherwise you could damage your ears. You can alter and control the filter sweeps using the intensity slider. You control the modulation rates with the speed slider.

Automatic Filter really is an extremely versatile tool and best understood by examining the various presets. Underwater sounds and wah-wah are specialities of the house. But once again, if you value your eardrums, go easy with the resonance slider!

Track Echo

Although echo is available as a send effect in GarageBand this one is track specific. The delay time is synced to your song tempo and you use the repeat slider to determine the number of echoes. If you want the echoes to become gradually darker move the colour slider to the left. For progressively brighter echoes, move the slider to the right. Once again, this is an example of low-

pass and highpass filtering. Use the intensity slider to control the volume of the repeat echo (not the original signal).

Chorus

Probably the most used effect of all time, particularly on guitar. How does it work? The audio signal is split into two signals. One is delayed and subjected to various degrees of pitch modulation before being mixed in with the

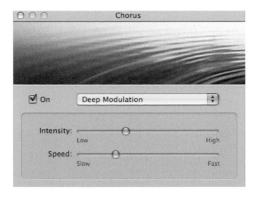

original, dry, signal. GarageBand's chorus is simplicity itself. Use the intensity slider to increase the depth of chorus and the speed slider to alter the modulation rate. It's most effective on polyphonic instruments like guitar or piano and produces a rich, fat, swirling sound.

Flanger

Very similar to chorus but with an extra control slider for feeding the processed signal back into its own input. In other words the processed audio is processed a second time. The result is an undulating effect, similar in character to the sounds produced by the Automatic Filter. Flanging is typically used on guitar but you can use it on just about anything, even drums.

Phaser

This is another classic modulation effect, sometimes confused with flanging. GarageBand's phaser controls are identical to the flanger but the effect is smoother, more musical and less metallic.

Tremolo

A favourite with guitarists since the 60s, tremolo is achieved by modulating the volume of the signal not its pitch. It's simple to use, with speed and intensity sliders. As a mono effect it's not particularly spectacular sounding but

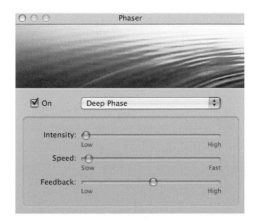

tick the auto pan box and it really comes to life. Now you'll hear the signal in stereo as it alternates between the left and right speakers. The speed is synced to your song tempo.

Auto-Wah

Wah-wah was invented to help guitar players imitate the classic talking effect produced by trumpet and trombone players when they use a plunger mute. Of course, guitarists can't use plunger mutes. Instead they use a pedal to open and close a special filter. In GarageBand the filter is triggered automatically, according to the intensity of the signal. You can choose from six filters – thick, thin, peak and classic 1-3 – and alter the character of the sound and the intensity of the effect. Obviously you don't get the fine degree of control available with a foot pedal but nevertheless, interesting results can be achieved, depending on the source material. Start messing with the presets, to get a general idea of how it works.

Amp simulation

This is the GarageBand effect that gets the most attention, and understandably so, because you can choose between six classic guitar amplifier emulations – three British and three American – at the click of a mouse. Use the pre-gain control to increase your input signal. The further to the right you move the slider, the more distortion you get. Beneath the pre-gain slider you'll find three tone controls; low, mid and high. Use the presence control to lift the guitar in a muddy mix.

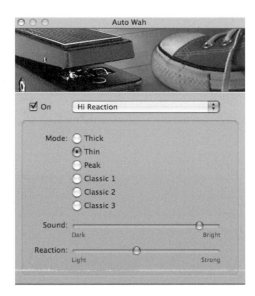

Speech Enhancer

New to version 3, this one's aimed at the growing number of podcasters using GarageBand. You can choose an optimised preset for your computer microphone, although, at the time writing, settings for the Pro range have yet to be added.

Four recording-type presets are available, two male and two female. A simple noise gate is also included here in the form of the Reduce Noise slider. Use it in same way as you would the Gate effect (mentioned earlier), to reduce background noise.

Vocal Transformer

If you like extreme vocal effects, this is the plug-in for you. The best results are obtained using a mono source, in other words, a single human voice. Editable parameters here are Pitch and Sound. Pitch is self-explanatory; to alter the pitch of your voice, just move the slider right (voice goes up) or left (voice goes down), in semitone increments. But what does the Sound slider do?

Select a preset, let's say, 'Male to Female' and something obvious happens; the voice pitch is raised by an octave and takes on a feminine character. But the Sound slider has also moved slightly, towards the High setting. The opposite happens if you select the 'Female to Male' preset. You see, the Sound slider is not a tone control, as the name implies, it actually changes the voice formants, the character of the human voice.

Info

If you find the GarageBand effects a bit limiting you can always use the Audio Unit effects that come bundled with OS X. They will appear in the insert list, immediately below the GarageBand effects.

Master effects

Still in the track info window, below the insert effects you'll see two more effects listed – Echo and Reverb. These are known as 'send' effects and are not totally track specific. Although you control the amount used on a particular track (using the slider) the actual type of reverb or echo effect chosen and their overall settings are determined in the Master Track. And where's that? Its settings are always available from the track info window. Just click the tab labelled Master.

Echo

In essence, this is the same as Track Echo, discussed earlier. So, if you intend applying it to more than one track at a time, making it available globally – here on the master track – will use less of your computer's processing power than inserting it on a track-by-track basis. Once you've established your master echo settings, return to the individual tracks to adjust the individual send levels.

Reverb

Last but certainly not least, this is the effect you will probably use the most. And that's the main reason for it being available globally. Reverb is used to simulate the acoustic environment of your music. Use the reverb time parameter to determine the size of your virtual space; the longer the setting, the larger the room. Use the colour slider to control the frequencies.

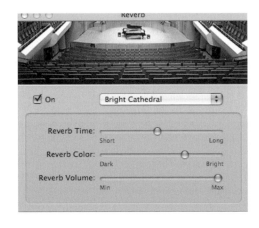

GarageBand has a large selection of rooms, halls and even cathedrals to choose from and using them as starting points is usually the best way to go.

For example, suppose you've composed and recorded a guitar based rock song. You wouldn't choose a cathedral simulation because rock bands sound awful playing in huge, empty buildings. It would better to select a 'medium hall' or 'live stage' preset instead and perhaps, tweak the parameters slightly. Alter them too much, though, and you might just as well start again, with a different preset.

Where should you place the volume slider? It doesn't really matter if you

leave the volume at maximum because you can set independent levels for each track. Once you've established your master reverb settings, return to the individual tracks to adjust the individual send levels.

Try these for size

There are a whole host of OS X Audio Unit Effects that you can also use in GarageBand. You'll find them listed beneath the GarageBand effects in the details section of the track info window. Here's a list and a very brief description of their functions.

- AUBandpass – a single-band bandpass filter.
- AUDynamicsProcessor – a dynamics processor that lets you set parameters such as headroom, the amount of compression, attack and release times, and so on.
- AUDelay – a delay unit.
- AUFilter – a five-band filter, allowing for low and high frequency cutoffs as well as three bandpass filters.
- AUGraphicEQ – a 10-band or 31-band graphic equalizer.
- AUHiPass – a high-pass filter with an adjustable resonance peak.
- AUHighShelfFilter – a filter that allows you to boost or cut high frequencies by a fixed amount.
- AUPeakLimiter – a peak limiter.
- AULowPass – a low-pass filter with an adjustable resonance peak.
- AULowShelfFilter – a filter that allows you to boost or cut low frequencies by a fixed amount.
- AUMultibandCompressor – a four-band compressor.
- AUMatrixReverb – a reverberation unit that allows you to specify spatial characteristics, such as size of room, material absorption characteristics, and so on.
- AUNetSend – a unit that streams audio data over a network. Used in conjunction with the AUNetReceive generator audio unit.
- AUParametricEQ – a parametric equalizer.
- AUSampleDelay – a delay unit that allows you to set the delay by number of samples rather than by time.
- AUPitch – an effect unit that lets you alter the pitch of the sound without changing the speed of playback.

Production

Drums first? Not always

Apple loops are a great way to kick start a new song and particularly useful for generating rhythm tracks. Most people start with a drum loop and work from the bottom up. But it isn't always the best way. After all how many hit songs do you remember purely on the strength of the drum parts?

Why not try out a few harmonic possibilities first; a guitar loop maybe or some simple piano chords. Starting with a simple chord sequence will establish a mood and may well generate melodic ideas for the lead vocal or instrumental line.

Finding suitable bass and drum loops to fit the music will now be much easier than arbitrarily selecting one from among the hundreds GarageBand has to offer.

Avoid musical conflict

Avoid loops that, when played together, are competing for musical space. A busy drum loop, for example, will often work better with a simple bass line and vice versa. A busy electric piano loop will likely complement a sparsely played guitar loop with spacey sounding chords.

This may sound obvious but thousands of beginners to music production make the elementary mistake of selecting busy, exciting loops that sound great on their own but messy when heard together.

The following four loops work well together.

Figure 10.1
All these loops come from GarageBand.

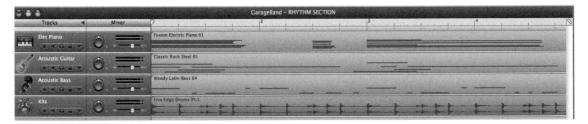

The four-bar example above contains only Apple loops that come with GarageBand. The Fusion Electric Piano 01 loop is uncluttered, leaving ample space for the busier arpeggios on the Classic Rock Steel 01 loop. The forceful sounding drum loop, Live Edgy Drums 05, contrasts well with the Woody Latin Bass 04 loop, which is sparsely played and relaxed in character.

QuickTip

Instrument loops that compete for similar frequencies in your production can sometimes be corrected at the mixing stage. However it's much easier, and quicker to sort it out here, at the production stage.

QuickTip

To avoid musical and frequency spectrum conflicts, as a rule of thumb, choose and mix together loops with opposite characteristics. Offset busy playing with sparse playing. Contrast hard kick drums with soft bass sounds and vice versa. Contrast bright, vibrant instrument loops with duller, mellower sounding ones.

Avoid middle frequency conflict

Avoid loops, too, that are competing for the same space in the audio frequency spectrum. It's usually more of a problem in the middle frequency area than the lower and higher ones. For example, you've found a rhythm guitar loop and a Rhodes piano loop that work well together musically. However they both contain chords in the same frequency range and the combined result sounds somewhat muddy.

A possible solution to the problem might be to transpose one of the loops up an octave, thereby immediately placing it in a higher frequency band.

Another solution might be to change the instrument type. For example, an acoustic grand piano will sound brighter and more distinctive than the Rhodes instrument, which has a mellower tone. Perhaps adding amp simulation will more readily distinguish the guitar from the piano.

Avoid low frequency conflict

Low frequency conflicts are less of a problem. The most frequent clash for space is between the bass and the kick drum. If you've chosen a drum loop with a tight kick drum sound, look for a bass loop with a softer, slower attack. Conversely, if you've chosen a drum loop with a loose sounding kick drum, search for a bass loop with a fast attack and a harder, more percussive character.

Mixing and matching

When mixing and matching piano, guitar or bass loops, listen carefully, to make sure the actual notes played fit with the other instruments. Even if your knowledge of musical theory is limited, you'll know instinctively if something sounds wrong. So hunt around until you find a loop that sounds correct. Using the Scale menu will help in this respect.

These two following screenshots demonstrate how changing the Scale option, from Major to Minor, filters the loop browser results.

But don't worry about mixing keys. If the notes in one loop are clashing with the notes of another, it's due to the actual harmonic structure of the music and has nothing to do with either loop's original key. GarageBand always transposes any loop you choose to fit the song's key.

Figure 10.2
244 major loops are available in the Rock/Blues category – scale Major.

Loops ⬍	Genres	Rock/Blues	Name ▲	Tempo	Key	Beats	Fav
All	Cinematic	Rock/Blues (244)	70s Ballad Drums 01	80	-	8	☐
By Genres	Country	Acoustic (163)	70s Ballad Piano 01	80	C	16	☐
By Instruments	Electronic	Acoustic Guitar (22)	70s Ballad Piano 02	80	C	16	☐
By Moods	Experimental	All (55)	70s Ballad Piano 03	80	C	8	☐
Favorites	Jazz	All Drums (94)	70s Ballad Piano 04	80	C	16	☐
	Orchestral	Bass (17)	70s Ballad Piano 05	80	C	16	☐
	Other Genre	Beats (1)	80s Pop Beat 07	110	-	8	☐
	Rock/Blues	Brass (3)	80s Pop Beat 08	110	-	16	☐
	Urban	Cheerful (106)	80s Pop Beat 09	110	-	16	☐
	World	Clean (180)	80s Pop Beat 10	110	-	16	☐
		Dark (6)	Acoustic Picking 09	78	D	8	☐
		Distorted (32)	Acoustic Picking 12	102	C	8	☐
		Dry (129)	Ambient Guitar 01	75	A	8	☐
		Elec Bass (17)	Barbeque Blues Long	-	-	00:37	☐
Scale: Major	Q-	244 items	Barbeque Blues Medium	-	-	00:24	☐

Figure 10.3
179 minor loops are available in the Rock/Blues category – scale Minor.

Tempo matching

Generally speaking, for conventional styles of music, matching loops will be easier if you keep them to similar tempo ranges. For example, a drum loop recorded at 125 bpm is more likely to sit well with a bass loop recorded at 140 bpm than another, recorded at 75 bpm. However, this is not a hard and fast rule. Sometimes, mixing and matching widely varying tempos can yield surprisingly good results. Use your own judgement.

From humble beginnings...

Beginners often drag a selection of loops onto the timeline and quickly run out of ideas. After repeating the loops a few times, things become very repetitive and boredom soon creeps in. An introduction can help get your tune off to an interesting start.

Skilled arrangers often write an intro last, taking various bits of material from the finished tune and reworking them as an intro. An easier way is to use the 'let's introduce the rhythm section' method. Countless soul bands have used it over the years, to introduce members of the band on stage. And the same technique is commonly heard on modern day dance music tracks.

Any instrument can start but it's usually the drums, followed by bass. Once a groove is established, the guitar and electric piano join the fray, one after the other. In the screenshot below, four 4-bar loops have been used to create a 20-bar song introduction simply by introducing them to the listener one at a time.

> ### QuickTip
>
> If you find a software loop that very nearly fits your existing loops but one or two notes don't match, why not use it anyway and simply alter the offending notes in the editor.

Figure 10.4
Four 4-bar loops have been used to create a 20-bar song intro.

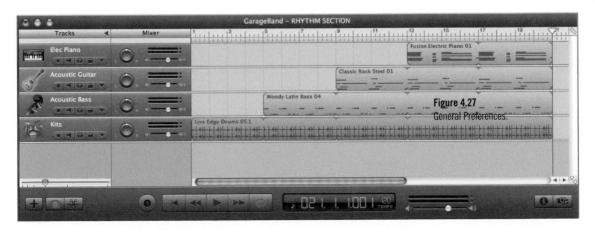

On form

Most music has form – a framework, often planned in advance. Casual listeners don't often notice form, nor should they, because in most cases it's a hidden element. They enjoy the music on a superficial level, and quite rightly so. After all, when we gaze at a splendid work of art we are not necessarily examining the hidden form. We appreciate the whole picture.

Sometimes, the musical form is very simple, a 12-bar blues, for example. Sometimes it's complex and stretches across a long time span, a classical symphony, for example. Most readers of this book will be more concerned with pop song structure.

Pop songs are varied in their structure. However, one form seems to be more pre-dominant than most and usually contains a verse (A), a chorus (B) and a bridge (C). Verses and choruses are a bit like questions and answers. The verse makes a statement and the chorus answers it. The verse is not always particularly memorable (but it's better if it is). However, the chorus is always stronger with a very memorable melody.

The most common way to start a song, after the introduction, is to repeat the verse and chorus – A B A B. But even the strongest verse and chorus becomes repetitive after a couple of minutes and most songwriters then add a bridge – A B A B C. To provide a contrast, this bridge section often departs from the main key of the song. After that the song usually continues with another chorus or two, A B A B C B B. This structure varies considerably. For example, you could repeat the verse before introducing the chorus – A A B A B C B B.

Repetition and variation

Memorable tunes rely heavily on repetition. How else can people remember them? They expect repetition. It's a subconscious human desire. Your listeners will rapidly lose interest in your tunes if you don't repeat anything. The danger then, of course, is predictability, especially if you're relying heavily upon loops. To alleviate boredom in a repeated section experienced composers use a technique known as repetition and variation.

Listen to any type of popular music – dance music, rock music, country music, techno and so on – and you'll hear subtle melodic and rhythmic changes every eight or maybe sixteen bars. Very often it's the addition or subtraction of a percussion instrument like a tambourine or claves, or the introduction of an instrumental riff. It's these changes that maintain the listeners interest, often without them ever realizing why.

Layering tracks

If your production is sounding full, on a musical level, but texturally thin, why not try out track layering. All you have to do is duplicate a software instrument track and assign it to another instrument. Choose a contrasting instrument for maximum effect and clarity.

In the first example opposite, the rather soft sounding acoustic bass track was duplicated and reassigned to a punchy grand piano instrument. It was then transposed down an octave. In the second example, a synth layer – Negrill Sweep – was added to the electric piano. Both tracks were then panned off-centre a bit. The resulting sound was huge and exciting, compared to the first version.

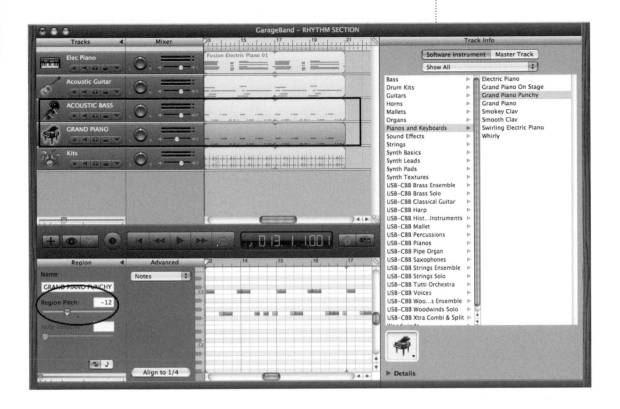

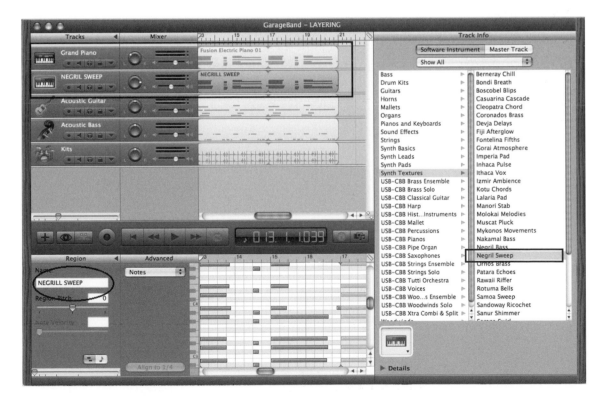

QuickTip

After double tracking a solo instrument pan the tracks right and left for a wide stereo effect. For vocals though, it's usually best to leave both tracks in the centre of the stereo picture.

Double tracking

Double tracking was a favourite technique for thickening vocal takes back in the days of analogue tape recording. It's simple enough to do. You just sing the song twice, taking care to keep as close to the original part as possible. Of course, the second take will never be quite the same as the first, but it's the small timing discrepancies that make it such an appealing effect. This technique also works well on solo instruments such as guitar and saxophone.

Join forces

Computer music production can be a solitary business. It certainly was with the first version of GarageBand because you couldn't record a complete band. However, although simultaneous multitrack recording in GarageBand is now possible many people reading this book will still be working alone. But it's not always the best way. Writing, producing and mixing entire songs is a tall order for experienced professionals, let alone beginners and hobbyists. Professionals have help, band members, producers, engineers, A&R people, managers and so on. We al need a fresh pair of ears occasionally.

Forge partnerships with like-minded musicians. Ask them round to your studio or take your work to them, on a MacBook. And if you don't have any terrestrial musical friends, seek out the virtual variety, on the Internet. There are plenty of talented people out there with whom you can share your ideas. All you've got to do is export your work to iTunes and email it to them. They can then import the file into their software, add tracks and loops and bring new life and fresh ideas to the production. The old saying, 'two heads are better than one', holds true when it comes to music production.

Mixing and mastering

People approach 'mixing' in different ways, depending upon the types of productions they happen to be working on. A typical GarageBand production will contain, on average, about eight tracks, maybe a couple more. That takes into account two tracks for drums and percussion, bass, guitar, keyboards and lead vocal. Any remaining tracks will likely be assigned to strings, harmony vocals, instrumental riffs or solos and maybe some extra percussion. So where do you start?

Return to square one

Typically, a professional recording engineer carries out his mixing tasks using a special recording console. This will be fitted with a set of vertical volume faders, as opposed to GarageBand's horizontal sliders. And one of the first things he would do is pull all the track faders down. So before you do anything else, drag all the volume sliders in the track mixer to the left. This will effectively mute the playback of the entire song. Set the master volume slider at 0.0 dB. It's also a good idea to return all pan settings to the centre (Figure 11.1).

Bottom up

When mixing, it's common practice to work from the bottom upwards. As rule of thumb, start with your drum and percussion loops and then add bass, keyboards/guitar and other instruments, in that

Figures 11.1 and 11.2

QuickTip

You can set the master volume slider at 0.0 dB by option clicking on your computer keyboard.

Info

dB is short for decibel. The loudness of sound is measured in decibel units.

QuickTip

If you can't rotate the pan control knob, it must be locked. Turn off the track pan curve to enable manual operation of the pan control.

97

order. Finally add the lead vocal and backing harmonies.

Introduce and work on each track one at a time. Keep in mind the need for a satisfactory balance between them. No single element should completely dominate the others. Don't raise the faders too far. Give yourself room for manoeuvre, either up or down (Figure 11.2).

Where to pan

On a conventional drum kit the kick and snare drums are placed in the centre of the mix. The remainder of the kit, toms, hi-hat and cymbals are panned left and right, to reflect the real life positioning of the kit. If you're working with a MIDI loop, you can map the individual drums across several tracks and pan each one accordingly. If you're working with an audio drum loop it will most likely have been recorded in stereo anyway, so leave the pan control in the centre position.

Bass stays in the centre, for reasons of balance. So, too, does the lead vocal.

Apart from that, there are no rules. It makes sense, though, to place similar sounding instruments on opposite sides of the stereo picture. Instruments of a similar frequency are best separated, too. In the screenshot above, the piano is placed on the left and the guitar, on the right.

A clean slate

A professional engineer usually starts with a clean slate, without flattering effects like reverb and echo. But many of the GarageBand loops are set up with effects in place. On some loops this is okay. For example, a synthesizer preset will not sound the same if the effects are removed. But if send effects like reverb or echo are present on a drum or bass loop it's usually best to remove them. Then you can concentrate on the true sounds of the actual instruments. If reverb really is necessary, you can replace it later, towards the end of the mixing process.

Dynamic effects like compression and EQ can usually be left in place, as starting points for further adjustment.

Try the OS X Audio Unit Effects

When processing an audio drum loop with dynamic effects, you'll probably not be able to get at the individual drum hits. You'll have to settle for applying EQ and compression to the entire loop.

Now, GarageBand's compressor works well enough but it's a simple, single slider affair. For better results call up the AUDynamics processor. You'll find it amongst a whole list of OS X Audio Unit Effects (Details section, Track Info window).

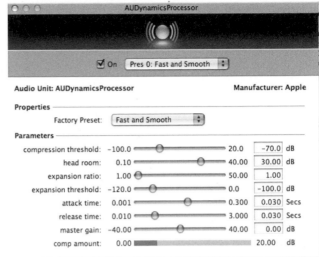

Figure 11.3
The AUDynamicsProcessor lets you set parameters such as headroom, the amount of compression, attack and release times, and so on..

Bass boom

If you've chosen your bass loops wisely, at the production stage, you shouldn't encounter problems getting them to blend with the kick drum. However, if you've recorded a bass guitar, some further work may have to be done. The most common problem is an overpowering bass with a tendency to boom. To cure this, try the Bass Reduction plug-in; it's effective and simple to use.

If that doesn't do the trick try EQ, starting with the Reduce Bass Boom preset.

QuickTip

Compressing a bass guitar at the mix-down will add punch and clarity to the sound as well as smoothing out unevenly played notes.

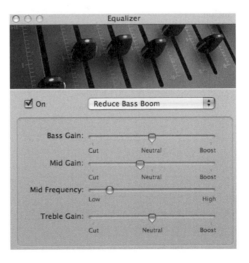

The midrange instruments

Getting keyboards and guitar to sit in the mix can be tricky. Taking one instrument at a time, raise the sliders until a satisfactory level is achieved. Generally speaking, they shouldn't be a lot louder or softer than the bass and drums.

Drastic EQ is usually unnecessary. After all, you don't want to destroy the very sound that you've either carefully chosen, as a loop, or the recorded sound of your instrument.

Bass and treble reduction, as opposed to boosting, is most always the right course of action. However, in a busy mix, a judicious boosting of the treble frequencies is sometimes required to clarify certain instruments. If two instruments are competing for space, panning them to opposite sides can be very effective.

Remember, no matter how well played, keyboards and rhythm guitar are playing a supporting role to the lead vocal or lead instrument, so keep the volume, echo and reverb levels to a sensible level.

The melodic thread

I mentioned earlier that no single element in the mix should completely dominate the others. That's true, but of course, the main melodic thread throughout your production - the lead vocal, instrumental solos and so on - should be centre stage and upfront.

Vocals will almost always benefit from a touch of reverb. I say a 'touch' because beginners so often saturate the singer with reverb and echo. All that does is give the vocal a far-away effect, which is the opposite of what's usually required - an upfront vocal. In the end it's a matter of taste and style. Some people like dry in-your-face vocals and others prefer wet, distant sounding voices.

Endless tweaking

As you've probably discovered, many of GarageBand's instruments come with pre-configured effects settings, individually tailored to suit the instrument in question. But on mix-down, when all the individual tracks are listened to as a whole, some of the effects may require adjustment. Fortunately, when you record with GarageBand's effects turned on, the audio itself remains dry, leaving you free to alter the settings as you mix.

Take stock

Once you've achieved an overall balance take stock and listen to the track as a complete entity. However, before you start adding the frills, take a long break. If you have the time and the patience, return to it a day or two later with fresh ears.

The final touches

On your return, listen critically. You'll almost certainly wish to make a few adjustments to the volume, EQ and effects. Before you do, though, make a backup copy of the current mix, in case you go down the wrong path.

If necessary, make minor volume adjustments using the track automation (volume curve). This is handy for fading instruments in and out at critical points in the song, rather than having abrupt entries and endings.

Figure 11.4
Use track automation to make those final volume level adjustments.

The master track

As mentioned earlier, a professional recording engineer typically carries out his mixing tasks using a special recording console. As well as individual channel strips and faders for each track, a recording console has a master section, with it's own dedicated master fader.

GarageBand's Master Track is the virtual equivalent of a hardware mixer's master section. All your individual tracks pass through here before being sent to iTunes as a two-track stereo mix-down. Unlike the instrument tracks it doesn't have a volume knob. But it does contain a volume curve. In most cases, once you've set your overall master volume you'll probably only use the master track's volume curve to create fade-outs at the end of some types of songs.

QuickTip

iLife can be used to create group mixes. For example, you could use it to create a backing vocal sub-mix, save it (as an iLife preview) and import it into another version of the same song. You will then have your backing vocals on their own pre-mixed stereo track, making the final mix-down much easier to handle (for details see Chapter 2, Working methods, iLife Previews).

Info

As well as controlling the volume of an entire song, the master track can also be used to transpose complete sections of your tunes when you select Master Pitch. Transposing parts of a song will help add variety to your productions.

Mastering Tools

You've already discovered that the echo and reverb parameters are determined in the master track info window. However, cast your eyes lower and you'll see another blank insert slot, an equaliser and a compressor slider. But EQ and compression facilities are available on the instrument tracks, so what are these for?

You can use these extra effects to add a final touch of gloss to your mix. Just as you might have used compression to add punch to a bass track, you now have the opportunity to do the same across the entire mix but only, of course, if it needs it. A number of excellent presets are available to get you started, although there is a caveat (see the quick tip below).

Warning

The GarageBand mastering presets contain reverb and echo settings, not what you'll always want if you've already set up your own. Make a note of your settings before applying the preset. You can then return to your original effects settings afterwards and keep or tweak the EQ and compression settings.

QuickTip

Don't limit yourself to mastering presets that relate just to your own particular style of music. Try them all. You never know, some of the more outrageous settings might just make your song stand out from the crowd.

The mastering tools are an excellent way to polish your stereo tracks before exporting them to iTunes or recording them to an external DAT or CD recorder. The presets will give you some idea of how it works.

For example, the Jazz Basic preset adds a touch of compression to the mix. Load the Jazz Club setting, however, and you'll see (and hear) that the mid frequencies have been boosted somewhat, to brighten the mix. I recommend starting with these presets and adjusting the effects to suit your own style of music.

In GarageBand, the term 'mastering' refers to the insertion of EQ and compression, to polish the master track during the final mix-down process.

Professional polish up

If you feel confident enough to polish your mix with a more professional mastering tool, try the AUMultibandCompressor, one of the Audio Unit plug-ins that are supplied with OS X.

Info

Confusion surrounds the term 'mastering'. In the recording industry, professional mastering engineers work with special equipment and software in dedicated mastering suites. It's a post-mix process. Entire albums are mastered this way to achieve a level of consistency across all the tracks.

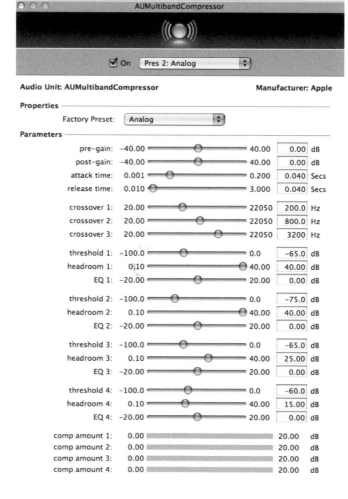

Info

Multiband compressors are used to split the incoming audio signal into separate frequency bands (in the case of Apple's AUMultibandCompressor, four frequency bands) before compression is applied. This enables you to raise the overall volume of a piece of music by compressing only those frequencies that actually need it. A good deal of careful listening is involved when using it.

Testing testing

Before you make a final decision about your mix, burn a CD or export your song to iTunes. Now play it on as many stereo systems as possible, including over headphones, and take notes. If it sounds consistently good across a wide range of consumer hi-fi gear, you're on track.

Upgrade your monitors

If your mixes sound good in your studio and poor on your other stereo equipment, it's probably your monitor speakers that are the root cause. Cheap computer speakers are designed to flatter the sound and will not provide an accurate picture. Invest in the most expensive pro audio speakers that you can afford.

Fortunately good budget reference monitors are becoming increasingly common. The Resolv range from Samson Audio for example are good value for money. Three hundred pounds will buy a pair of their Resolv 60a powered speakers which produce a full sound with a transparent mid-range. M-Audio also manufactures reasonably priced reference monitors called the Studiophile range.

A pair of studio reference monitors like the Samson Resolv 6a will help you create accurate mixes

Ready to go

Once you're satisfied with the mix, exporting it to iTunes is simplicity itself. From the file menu, select 'Export to iTunes'. Before you do so, check the master level meters. Are they clipping (showing red) at any point in the song? If so, reduce the volume in the master track a little or maybe apply a small amount of compression to the mix. After exporting the song, you can play it in iTunes along with all the pro stuff you may have downloaded from the iTunes music store.

Podcasting

If you're running GarageBand 3 you can't fail to have noticed the new podcasting facilities. Podcasts are broadcast on the Internet, like a radio or television show. However, radio and television episodes are usually broadcast at regular intervals. Podcasts, on the other hand, can be downloaded at any time and listened to in iTunes or on an iPod at a time that suits the listener.

Plan a format

You can create your own podcast episodes in GarageBand and then upload them to the Internet using iWeb or similar software. Before you do though, work out a scheme. Radio shows work to set formats with signature tunes, intros, various topics, interviews, background music and conclusions. Listen to a few radio shows that you like, jot down their formats, and then devise your own.

Short and sweet

Start small and aim for about 20-minutes of content rather than a long drawn out episode that might bore the pants off your listeners. When you're more confident, you can stretch out a bit. Also, limit your topics to 5 minutes or so. A 15-minute episode, for example, could look like this:

- Spoken intro – what you and your podcast is all about – 60 seconds
- Signature tune – something recognizable, with which to start each and every episode – 30 seconds
- First Topic – 5 minutes, 30 seconds
- Musical link – 30 seconds
- Second Topic – 5 minutes, 30 seconds
- Conclusion – thanks your listeners, guests, preview next episode and so on – 90 seconds.
- Signature tune – 30 seconds.

Of course, it needn't be done this way. For example, a more conventional method would be to place the signature tune at the beginning, before the spoken intro. Experiment and devise your own plan.

QuickTip

The playhead lock button (tiny mauve triangle) is set at 30 seconds when you open the default New Podcast Episode. To extend the episode, move the lock button to the right.

Figure 12.1
The Playhead Lock Button is a miniscule mauve triangle. Move it left or right, to extend or shorten the episode.

Ducking and diving

Avoid embarrassing gaps and keep things flowing. As a topic ends, fade up a short piece of music. When you begin the next topic, fade the music down again. An easy way to do this is to use the Ducking feature.

In Figure 12.2, ducking has been applied to the Jingles track (downward pointing arrow glows blue). As the host nears the end of the introduction his signature tune begins to play. However, because the host track is controlling the ducking (upward pointing arrow glows yellow), the music remains suppressed until he stops talking. Only then does the music rise in volume.

Figure 12.2
Ducking applied to Jingles track.

Look, no hands

Podcasting is all about talking and to make good quality recording you'll need a decent microphone. The Samson C01USB (see Chapter 4, Audio recording, Recording vocals) is a good choice.

Something else you'll need is a desktop stand. The C01USB, for example, can be used with a desktop stand and spider mount, for rumble-free easy no-hands recording.

Figure 12.3
The Samson C01 USB mic complete with desktop stand and spider mount.

Common practice

Use the Gate, to cut out background noise when you aren't speaking. Use the Compressor to smooth your overall vocal performance.

Remember this

- You adjust the input level of your voice using the gain control of your audio interface – not the volume slider in the GarageBand track mixer (refer to chapter 5, Audio recording, Your own input, for details).
- Always turn off your speakers and use headphones when you're recording with a microphone. If you don't, the sounds from the speakers will be recorded along with your voice.

Jingle all the way

Pro broadcasters use specially prepared jingles as signature tunes. And writing and arranging them is a skilled business. Fortunately though, GarageBand 3 has its own selection of copyright-free jingles. If you're not musically inclined, these jingles are an easy way to add a professional touch to your podcasts, without worrying about breaking copyright law.

As well as long, medium and short jingles, short stingers and sound effects can also be found in the loop browser.

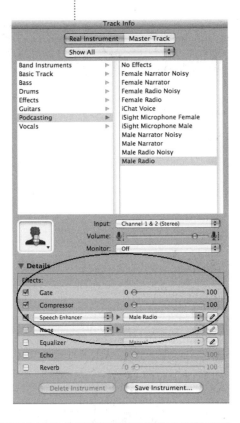

Blogg off

When your podcast is finished and nicely balanced, export it to iTunes and convert it to an AAC file. You can then publish your podcast using services such as www.blogger.com.

To broadcast on iTunes, you'll need to create an RSS file from your blog. To find out more visit www.apple.com/itunes/store/podcaststechspecs.html.

Appendix
Keyboard shortcuts

Action	Shortcut
Playback and Navigation	
Start or stop playback	Space bar
Go to beginning	Return or Z or Home
Go to end	Option-Z or End
Move back one measure	Left arrow
Move forward one measure	Right arrow
Move back the visible width of the timeline	Page up
Move forward the visible width of the timeline	Page down
Zoom out	Control-Left arrow
Zoom in	Control-Right arrow
Tracks	
Create a new track	Command-Option-N
Create a new Basic track	Command-Shift-N
Duplicate the selected track	Command-D
Delete the selected track	Command-Delete
Select the next higher track	Up arrow
Select the next lower track	Down arrow
Mute/Unmute the selected track	M
Solo/Unsolo the selected track	S
Show/Hide the track's volume and pan curves	A
Show/Hide the master track	Command-B
Show/Hide the podcast track	Command-Shift-B
Show/Hide the video track	Command-Option-B
Track Info pane	
Show/Hide the Track Info pane	Command-I
Select the next higher category or instrument	Up arrow (when the Track Info pane is open and a category or instrument is selected)
Select the next lower category or instrument	Down arrow (when the Track Info pane is open and a category or instrument is selected)

Action	Shortcut
Move from instrument list to category list	Left arrow (when the Track Info pane is open and an instrument is selected)
Move from category list to instrument list	Right arrow (when the Track Info pane is open and a category is selected)

Editing and Arranging

Action	Shortcut
Undo	Command-Z
Redo	Command-Shift-Z
Cut	Command-X
Copy	Command-C
Paste	Command-V
Delete	Delete
Select all	Command-A
Split selected region	Command-T
Join selected regions	Command-J
Snap to grid	Command-G
Enable/Disable ducking	Command-Shift-F

Recording

Action	Shortcut
Start or stop recording	R
Turn the cycle region on/off	C
Turn the metronome on/off	Command-U
Turn count in on/off	Command-Shift-U
Show/Hide instrument tuner	Command-F

Notation View

Action	Shortcut
Move selected notes to previous grid position	Left arrow
Move selected notes to next grid position	Right arrow
Move selected notes back one measure	Shift-Left arrow
Move selected notes forward one measure	Shift-Right arrow
Transpose selected notes up one semitone	Up arrow
Transpose selected notes down one semitone	Down arrow
Transpose selected notes up one octave	Shift-Up arrow
Transpose selected notes down one octave	Shift-Down arrow

Adjusting Master Volume

Action	Shortcut
Raise master volume	Command-Up arrow
Lower master volume	Command-Down arrow

Showing Windows and Editors

Action	Shortcut
Show track mixer	Command-Y
Show Track Info pane	Command-I
Show editor	Command-E
Show loop browser	Command-L
Show/Hide Media Browser	Command-R

Action	Shortcut
Show onscreen keyboard	Command-K
Show Musical Typing window	Command-Shift-K
File menu commands	
Create new project	Command-N
Open an existing project	Command-O
Close the current project	Command-W
Save the current project	Command-S
Save As	Command-Shift-S
Application menu commands	
Show/Hide GarageBand Preferences	Command-comma (,)
Hide GarageBand	Command-H
Hide other applications	Command-Option-H
Quit GarageBand	Command-Q
Help menu commands	
Open GarageBand Help	Command-question mark (?)

Index